Women Role Models

By the same author

—The Legend Makers

—Women's Higher Education in the 19th Century

About the Author

Gouri Srivastava is a Reader in Education at the Department of Women's Studies, National Council of Educational Research and Training (NCERT), New Delhi. She did her M.A and M.Phil from Jawaharlal Nehru University with high grade points. Her Ph.D is from Delhi University. Dr. Srivastava has published widely in academic journals and is the author of the following books: Women Who Created History, Women's Higher Education in the 19th Century, Education in India : A Historical Perspective, The Legend Makers: Some Eminent Muslim Women of India, Women's Education in India : Issues and Dimensions and the Role of Begums of Bhopal in Educating Girls' in the mid 19th & 20th Centuries. She is a recipient of scholarships from prestigious organisations such as Indian Council of Historical Research (ICHR) and Indian Council of Social Science Research (ICSSR) for completing her doctoral work.

Women Role Models

Some Eminent Women of Contemporary India

Gouri Srivastava

CONCEPT PUBLISHING COMPANY, NEW DELHI-110059

Cataloging in Publication Data—DK
Courtesy: D.K. Agencies (P) Ltd. <docinfo@dkagencies.com>

Srivastava, Gouri, 1961-
Women role models : some eminent women of contemporary India/ Gouri Srivastava.
p. cm.
Includes bibliographical references (p.)
Includes index.
ISBN 8180693368

1. Women—India—Biography. 2. Celebrities— India—Biography. I. Title.

DDC 920.720 954 22

ISBN 81-8069-336-8

First Published 2006

Published and Printed by
Ashok Kumar Mittal
Concept Publishing Company
A/15-16, Commercial Block, Mohan Garden
New Delhi-110059 (India)
Phones: 25351460, 25351794
Fax: 091-11-25357103
E-mail: publishing@conceptpub.com

Preface

The present book gives a vivid account of women who have made their mark in different fields. These women came from diverse socio-econmic backgrounds. Their journey towards attaining their goal is an inspirational account that can motivate both boys and girls for all times to come.

The book highlights the contributions of these women in different fields.

I express my heart felt gratitude to my family members who have always been a tremendous source of motivation and help. They have always been pillars of my strength in testing times.

I would also like to thank all the members and staff of the National Archives at Delhi, Nehru Memorial Museum and Library, the Central Secretariat Library, NCERT Library and the Library at the All Indian Women's Conference.

Gouri Srivastava

Contents

Introduction

India has a rich legacy of eminent women who have contributed to different fields. These women belonged to various communities and came from very diverse backgrounds. Their trials and successes in their journey of excelling in different fields have been briefly portrayed in the present book.

About twenty-six women who have contributed in diverse fields such as education, social service, fine arts, music and dance, literature, sports and freedom struggle have been projected. An account of their lives can be a great source of inspiration to both boys and girls for all times to come. It would also inculcate in them certain human values of caring and sharing, thus enabling them to value each other's contribution. In the context of the girl child, these women can be role models whom they can emulate or derive inspiration from. Perhaps, it would kindle in them a desire to achieve and perform something in life and also tread those areas that were earlier considered as male bastions.

These biographies of eminent women can be used as an exemplary material by the textbook writers and teachers for undoing the gender bias and stereotyping prevalent in the society. It would also help in translating some of the parameters of National Policy on Education 1986, which has a special section on—Education for women's Equality. The Para states the following:

4.2 Education will be used as an agent of basic change in the status of woman. In order to neutralise the accumulated distortions of the past, there will be a well-conceived edge in favour of women. The National Educational System will play a positive, interventionist role in the empowerment of women. It will foster the development of new values through redesigned curricula, textbooks, training and orientation of teachers, decision makers and administrators, and the active involvement of educational institutions. This will be an act of faith and social engineering. Women studies will be promoted as a part of various courses and educational institutions encouraged to take up active programmes to further women's development.

4.3 The removal of women's illiteracy and obstacles inhibiting their access to and retention in elementary education will receive overriding priority, through provision of special support services, setting of time targets, and effective monitoring. Major emphasis will be laid on women's participation in vocational, technical and professional education at different levels. The policy of nondiscrimination will be pursued vigorously to eliminate sex stereo typing in vocational and professional courses and to promote women's participation in nontraditional occupations, as well as in existing and emergent technologies.

Source: National Policy on Education—1986, p. 10

Besides helping in translating the policy parameters into reality, a biographical account of eminent women would also empower the girl child in her journey of attaining womanhood.

Asima Chatterjee

Awarded D.Sc. by the University of Calcutta in 1944
Nominated Member of Rajya Sabha during 1982-84
Re-nominated to Rajya Sabha in 1984
Awarded Sir Shanti Swarup Bhatnagar Award in 1961
Padma Bhushan in 1975
C.V. Raman Award for Physcial Science by UGC, 1982 in 1985

Asima Chatterjee was born on 23rd September, 1917 at Calcutta. She received her early education in this city. Her parents were Dr. Indra Narayan Mukherjee and Smt. Kamla Devi. She underwent her school education in Bethune Collegiate School from 1925-32 and in Bethune College from 1932-34; B.Sc, M.Sc and D.Sc in Calcutta University from 1934-36, 1936-38 and 1938-44 respectively. She was awarded D.Sc by the University of Calcutta in 1944 on the merit of her thesis, "The Chemistry of Plant Products". She carried out her post doctoral research from University of Wisconsin, USA in 1947-48 under Professor L.M. Parks; California Institute of Technology, Pasadena, USA and under from Prof. L. Zechmeister in 1948-49, and University of Zurich, Switzerland under Prof. P. Karrer in 1949-1950. She started her teaching career in 1940 at the Lady Brabourne College, Calcutta, where she served as Professor and Head of the Department of Chemistry till 1954 when she joined as Reader in Chemistry at the University College of Science, Calcutta. She was appointed Khaira Professor of Chemistry in 1962. While at the Lady Brabourne College she also served as a lecturer at the University College of Science.

She was actively engaged in research since 1937 and made significant contributions in the fields of alkaloids, terpenoids, coumarins, organic analytical chemistry and reaction mechanism.

The main focus of her work has been alkaloids, poly phenolics and terpenoids. Her pioneering work on the alkaloids of Alstonia,

Kopsia, Rauwolfia, Rhyzya and Vinca had considerable impact on the subsequent research in the field of indole alkaloids in India and abroad. Professor Asima Chatterjee has investigated the Chemistry of almost all the principal types of indole alkaloids known today. She has made notable contributions to the elucidation of the structure and stereochemistry of ajmalicine and sarpagine. A landmark achievement was the isolation and characterisation of gessoschizine, a key precursor in the biogenesis of indole alkaloids from Rhyzya Stricta.

Besides fundamental research on the Chemistry of indole alkaloids, Professor Asima Chatterjee has made significant contribution to the Chemistry of Steroidal alkaloids, particularly, on the novel 5L–pregnane derivatives isolated from Aocynaceae and Buxaceae. A simplified and normal procedure of the preparation of the required beta-phenyle thanolamines in connection with alkaloid synthesis was developed by her. Attention was also given to synthesis of these alkaloids under physiological conditions.

Professor Chatterjee has been a member of many professional bodies (learned societies) such as Sigma XI of USA, Indian Chemical Society, Indian Association for the Cultivation of Science, Indian Science Congress Association, Indian Academy of Science Educational Board, Indian Journal of Chemistry and Chemical Society (London).

Professor Asima Chatterjee has been bestowed with many awards, honours and distinction for her notable contributions in the field of science. She received Nagarjuna Gold Medal in 1940, Prem Chand Rychand Studentship in 1942, Mout Medal in 1944, and Bhuban Mohini Dasi Gold Medal in 1981 from Calcutta University; Watumull Fellowship of USA in 1948-49; Shanti Swarup Bhatnagar Prize in 1961; INSA Fellow in 1961; Woman of the Year and Silver Medal by Bengal Chamber of Commerce in 1975; President of Indian Science Congress in 1975; Sir C.V. Raman Award by UGC in 1982; Sisir Kumar Mitra Memorial Award of INSA in 1984; Sir Asutosh Mukherjee Gold Medal by Indian Science Congress in 1989; Goyal Foundation Gold Medal in 1992; Padma Bhushan in 1975. She has edited many publications such as Bharater Bonousadhi

(In Bengali, 6 Volumes, University of Calcutta, 1973); Treatise on 'Indian Medicinal Plants'. (6 Volumes, CSIR); and served as editor of Indian Chemical Society and was a member of the editorial board of Indian Journal of Chemistry.

Professor Asima Chatterjee was a nominated member of Rajya Sabha (1982-84, 1984-90); Union Public Service Commission (UPSC); UGC and CSIR; Ministry of Health and Family Welfare and many other important state and national level bodies.

For the Users

This is the story of a women scientist who received various prestigious awards for her contribution in the field of Chemistry. She was the recipient of the highest civilian award and also has the distinction of being nominated to the Rajya Sabha.

REFERENCES

Bagchi, K., Asoke (1994): *Great Women of Science,* Konarak Publishers, New Delhi.

Jain, C.K. (1993): *Women Parliamentarians in India,* Surjeet Publication, New Delhi.

Hansa Mehta

First among girls who appeared for the matriculation examination in 1913.
Elected to the Bombay Municipal Schools Committee in 1926.
Participated in the first conference of the A.I.W.C. held in Poona in 1927.
President of A.I.W.C. in 1945-46.
Member of the Senate, SNDT Women' University and its Syndicate till 1948 and Vice Chancellor from 1946 to 1948.
Member of the Government of India Secondary Education Commission in 1952-53.
Member of All India Council for Secondary Education in 1955.
President of Inter University Board of India in 1956.
Vice Chancellor of Maharaja Sayaji Rao University, Baroda from 1949 to 1958.
Member of the Executive Board of UNESCO—1956-60.

Hansa Mehta was born in Surat and was educated at Baroda. She had the distinction of standing first among girls who appeared for the matriculation examination in 1913, thus, winning the coveted Chalfied prize. She also won the Gangubai Bhatt Scholarship in the Inter Arts and later graduated with Honours in Philosophy from Bombay University.

She entered public life soon after her marriage to Dr. Jivraj N. Mehta, an eminent physician and administrator. In 1926, she was elected to the Bombay Municipal Schools Committee. She participated in the first conference of the A.I.W.C. held in Poona in 1927. At this conference, she strongly supported the resolution condemning early marriage of girls as this interfered with

* A.I.W.C—All India Women's Conference

their education. In the same year, she founded the Bombay Branch of the A.I.W.C. and became its first Secretary. She was the Vice President of the A.I.W.C. several times and was elected President in 1945-46.

She took an active part in the freedom struggle. Later, she became a member of the Constituent Assembly 1947-50. She gave evidence before the Parliamentary Committee led by Sir Pethick Lawrence regarding the reservation of seats for women in Parliment which she vehememtly opposed.

Smt. Mehta has made her mark as one of the foremost educationists in the country. In pre-independence India she was a member of several important educational institutions and left her mark in whatever she did.

In post-independence India she continued to hold important posts in the field of education. She was the Vice Chancellor of SNDT University, Bombay from 1946 to 1948. She was a member of the Government of India Secondary Education Commission (1952-53); Member of All India Council for Secondry Education (1955) and President of Inter University Board of India (1956). She was the founder member and Vice Chancellor of Maharaja Sayaji Rao University, Baroda and held this office from 1949 to 1958.

She is the holder of Hon. Degree of Doctor of Letters from the Allahabad University (1958) and of the M.S. University of Baroda (1959) and a Hon. L.L.B. from Leeds University, U.K. (1965).

She gave valuable suggestions regarding elementary education. Under her guidance the Hansa Mehta Committee made some significant suggestions i.e. common curricula for boys and girls at the elementary stage, with home science as a common core subject for both boys and girls at the middle stage. Further, for women teachers, the committee recommended that they should be appointed in boys' schools to encourage girls to join these institutions.

Smt. Mehta represented Government of India on many delegations abroad like the Nuclear Sub-Committee on the Status of Women of the U.N. (1946). Human Rights Commission of the U.N. from 1947 to 1952 of which she became the Vice Chairman in 1950-52. She was also the Indian Delegate to the Commonwealth Parliamentary Conference in 1948. As the President of the Indian Conference of Social Work (1954-57) she led the Indian Delegation to the 8th World Conference of Social Work at Munich (1956). She also led the Indian Delegation to the World Family Congress at Paris (1958).

Smt. Mehta has been closely associated with UNESCO. She was a member of the Indian Delegation to the UNESCO Conference - Delhi (1956), Member of the Executive Board of UNESCO (1956-60). In 1959, the Social Division of the U.N. invited her to work on the commission to examine social work conditions in member countries, and in 1954 the Executive Committee of the Commonwealth Universities invited her as representative of the Indian Universities Board in Canada.

As a prolific writer, her works include several books, stories for children, translation into Gujarati of Shakespeare's work (done in blankverse), translations of Molierie's work (for the Sahitya Academy—India). She translated into Gujarati Valmiki's Ramayan and several tracts and pamphlets including 'Women under the Hindu Law of Marriage and Succession, (1944), Tract on Post War Education Reconstruction (1945), Civil Liberties in 1945). For her immense contribution to education and for the welfare of women, the Government of India conferred on her the highest civilian award of Padma Bhushan in 1959.

For the Users

The noted educationist who had the distinction of being the first matriculate from Gujarat. She held various responsible positions in Government and non Government organisations. She was one of the members of the Government of India Secondary Education Commission.

REFERENCE

Volume on Diamond Jubilee 1927-87- All India Women's Conference, New Deihi.

Kalpana Chawla

First Indian women to go in to space - 1997.

Kalpana Chawla, on 19th November, 1997 became the first Indian woman to go into space when the US space shuttle Columbia blasted off from the Kennedy Space Centre at Cape Canaveral in Florida. The Karnal born 37 years old aerospace engineer, Kalpana was part of a 16- day research mission whose programme included the release of a freeflying satellite to study the sun and the first space walk by a Japanese astronaut.

Kalpana was born in Karnal on July 1st 1961. She started her education at the Tagore school, Karnal, India, from where she graduated in 1976. She later got her Bachelor of Science Degree in Aeronautical Engineering from Punjab Engineering College, India, 1982. Later on , she took her Master of Science Degree in Aerospace Engineering from University of Texas, 1984, and Doctorate of Philosophy in aerospace engineering from the University of Colorado, 1988. Her educational background speaks volumes about her determination and well set out goal for being an astronaut one day.

In 1988, Kalpana Chawla started her work at NASA Ames Research Centre in the area of powered-lift computational fluid dynamics. Her research concentrated on simulation of complex airflows encountered around aircraft such as the Harrier in "ground-effect". Following the completion of this project, she worked on several others. Further, she was responsible for the development and implementation of efficent techniques to perform aerodynamic optimisation. Results of her various projects are documented in technical conference papers and journals.

She was selected by NASA in December, 1994. She reported

to Johnson Space Centre in March, 1995 as an astronaut candidate in the 15th group of Astronauts.

In November,1996, Kalpana Chawla was appointed as mission specialist and prime robotic arm operator on STS-87 (November 19 to Decmber 5, 1997). STS-87 was the fourth U.S. Microgravity Payload flight and focused on experiments designed to study how the weightless environment of space affects various physical processes, and on observations of the Sun's outer atmospheric layers. Two members of the crew performed an EVA (space walk) which featured the manual captures of a Spartan satellite, in addition to testing EVA tools and procedures for future Space Station assembly. In completing her first mission, Kalpana Chawla travelled 6.5 million miles in 252 orbits of the Earth and logged 376 hours and 34 minuters in space. In January 1998, Kalpana Chawla was appointed as crew representative for shuttle and station flight crew equipment. Subsequently, she was appointed as the lead for Astronaut Officer's Crew Systems and Habitability Section. She was subsequently assigned to the crew of STS-107 scheduled for launch in 2003. On February 1, 2003, a fairy tale came to an end, when NASA's space shuttle Columbia desintegrated into flame, 63 kilometres above the ground after almost 16 perfect days in the orbit. Among those crew members who perished was Kalpana Chawla. She was 16 minutes from home; so near and yet so far. One of the last experiments conducted by her during the 16 day science mission of space shuttle Columbia was to study the physics of combustion.

Kalpana has become a legend at her home. Her life began in a small, tradition bound town in India and ended on a return from space. She broke all barriers to enter a unique vocation and be counted as a member of the world's most prestigious professions.

Recently, the University of Texas at Arlington has dedicated a new residential facility in the campus for students to the memory of astronaut Kalpana Chawla, who died in space shuttle Columbia crash in 2003.

For the user

This is a poignant story of a young woman who reached the space and set an example for her fellow beings.

REFERENCE

Gupta, R., Gupta Indra, *Kalpana Chawla:* A Fairy Tale Saga with a Tragic End, I Con Publications Pvt. Ltd, New Delhi, 2003.

Kanaka, Tanjore Santhanakrishna

Gradutated in Medicine from Madras University in 1954.
Obtained postgraduate degree in surgery in 1963.
Ph. D in Neurosurgery from Madras University in 1972.

Kanaka, Tanjore Santhanakrishna was born on 31st March, 1932. She became the first qualified woman neurosurgeon of India. She graduated in medicine from the Madras University in 1954. She later obtained her postgraduate degree in surgery in 1963 and Ph.D. in Neurosurgery in 1972 from Madras University. In 1964, she joined the Department of Neurology and Neurosurgery of the Madras Medical College and gradually became a leading neurosurgeon of India. She held the post of additional professor of neurosurgery at the Madras Medical College.

For the Users

This is the portrayal of a woman scientist who attained proficiency in the field of neurology and became the first woman to attain distinction in neurosurgery. She later on held faculty position at Madras Medical College.

REFERENCE

Bagchi, K. (Asoke, 1994) *Great Women of Science,* Konark Publishers, New Delhi.

Pradhan, Nita Basu

Graduated from Patna Medical College in 1962.

Nita Basu graduated from Patna Medical College in 1962 with the highest position and was awarded gold medal for her excellence in surgery. After her internship, she proceeded to the U.S.A. where she had training in neurosurgery, plastic surgery and cardiac surgery. Initially, she intended to be a plastic surgeon but later with encouragement from her teacher in Philadelphia she chose cardiac surgery as her field of specialisation. She spent ten years in the U.S.A., training in cardiac surgery before returning to India.

She successfully performed all types of cardiac operations except heart transplants. She was associated with the prestigious hospitals of Bombay like Breach Candy Hospital, and the Nanavati Hospital.

She had the distinction of being a Fellow of the American College of Surgeons and a Fellow of the Academy of Ophthalmology.

For the Users

A woman surgeon who had the distinction of being a Fellow of a reputed international organisation in America and association with the famous hospitals in Bombay.

REFERENCE

Bagchi, Asoke, (1994): Great women of science, Konark Publishers, New Delhi.

Lady Premleela Thackersey

Chairperson of the Kasturba Gandhi National Memorial Trust—1952-1972

Premleela Thackersey was the wife of the renouned educationist Sir Vithaldas Thackersey. She was educated upto school when she married Vithaldas. Like her husband, she was completely devoted to the cause of women's education. She constantly worked for the deprived and the down trodden. She was only 31when her husband passed away.

Premleela was determind to carry on her husband's charitable and philanthropic work. She used her beautiful mansion in Poona, Parnakuti, as a free boarding school and home for girls and women. These girls and women were supported by her family members. Premleela supervised this activity personally.

She was an ardent follower of Mahatma Gandhi. When Mahatma Gandhi undertook fast for 21 days for self-purification against untouchability she stood by him. She became the Chairperson of the Kasturba Gandhi National Memorial Trust in 1952 and continued in the office till 1972. She endeavoured to fulfil the dream of Gandhi, i.e.working for millions of poor women and children living in the rural India.

For the Users

A true Gandhian follower and a social worker who took up the cause of the helpless and downtrodden women.

REFERENCE

Nayar, Sushila and Mankekar Kamala (2002): *Women Pioneers in India's Renaissance: As I Remember Her*, National Book Trust, India.

Mridula Sarabhai

Worked in the Bal Sena of the Congress and the Shishu Vibhag of Akhil Bharat Charkha Sangh–1920-25.

Joined the Youth Movement under the leadership of Jawaharlal Nehru–1925-1930.

Was a Congress Seva Dal volunteer in the Freedom Movement, participating in the Salt Satyagraha, organising the boycott of foreign cloth and British goods–1930-1946.

Became the Organising Secretary, Kasturba Gandhi National Memorial Trust. She was a Shanti Sainik in Gandhi's programme of National and Emotional Integration –1945-1946.

In 1945, when Jawaharlal Nehru became the Congress President, he nominated Mridula as a member of the Congress Working Committee in 1946.

Worked with others in Bihar. Incharge of the peace mission and the rehabilitation of uprooted minorities –1946-1947.

She was the Convenor, Friends of New Kashmir Committee, which organised Delhi citizens resistance to communal movement in Kashmir–1950-1953.

She was the Convenor, Shanti Dal Delhi in 1953.

She was incharge of special rehabilitation schemes of the Jammu and Kashmir Government on behalf of the National Conference–1948-1953.

Became one of the secretaries of the Indian branch of Amnesty International, started in Indian in 1968-1974.

Mridula Sarabhai was born in a well-to-do family at Ahmedabad on May 6, 1911. Her parents were liberal and unconventional in their attitude. It is because of their constant encouragement and motivation that she did her initial schooling at 'The Retreat' the school run by her parents. Later she passed Vinit (equivalent to matriculation) in 1928 and joined Gujarat Vidyapeeth (the National Mahatma College) started by Gandhi. She passed the first year snatak course. Her involvement in the freedom struggle led to her discontinuance of college studies in 1930. She, however, did not loose track. She continued her self-education in jails and outside and during her apprenticeship with her parents, Shri Amdalal and Smt. Saraladevi Sarabhai, Jawaharlal Nehru and Mahatma Gandhi.

The above mentioned leaders constantly influenced her and made her fearless. In fact, at twenty she became a household name in Gujarat. The stories of her unusual courage and daring during the 1930's had spread throughout the province. She had the courage as well as qualities of a leader.

Her participation became more visible when she worked in Bal Sena of the Congress and the Shishu Vibhag of Akhil Bharat Charkha Sangh in 1920-25. Later, as a Congress Sevak Dal volunteer in the freedom movement, she participated in the salt satyagraha, organised the boycott of foreign cloth and British goods. She provided legal defence and did relief work for political workers and their families through organisations like Jyoti Sangh. She also specialised in the constructive programme of Quomi Ekta (communal harmony), Stree Jagriti and in Journalism.

In 1937, she participated in the Rajkot Satyagraha as a Praja Mandal volunteer. She held many distinguished positions e.g. she was a member, Municipal School Board, Ahmedabad in 1937-38. She was Acting Secretary, City Congress Committee, Ahmedabad 1941-42. During 1945-46, she became the Organising Secretary, Kasturba Gandhi National Memorial Trust. Later on, she was a Shanti Sainik in Gandhiji's programme of national and emotional integration. In 1916, when Jawaharlal Nehru became the Congress President, he nominated Mridula as a member of the Congress Working Committee and appointed her as one of the general secretaries of the Congress. This lasted until he became the Prime Minister of India in the Interim Government.

During the communal disturbances, she specialised in organising active resistance to them. She participated as a Shanti Sainik in bringing about normalcy during the following communal disturbances:

1941	—	Ahmedabad Communal Riots
1946	—	Garh Mukteshwar (Meerut)
1946-47	—	Bihar
1947-48	—	Punjab, both East and West
1948-50	—	Delhi
1961	—	Aligarh
1969	—	Ahmedabad

She was the Convenor, Friends of New Kashmir Committee which organised Delhi citizens resistance to the communal movement in Kashmir in 1950-53. She was also incharge of special rehabilitation schemes of the Jammu and Kashmir Government on behalf of the National Conference. She worked under the direction of Gopalaswami Ayyangar and Mirza Mohammed Afzal Beg and under the general guidance of Sheikh Mohammed Abdullah.

During this period (1948-53), the Congress leadership worked at cross purposes. One section, inspired by Jawaharlal, was more secular in its approach, while the other was inspired by pro-Hindu and anti-Pakistan sentiments. Through her activities, Mridula exposed and resisted these elements within the Congress and in the government.

In 1953, she came into conflict with disruptive and vested interests within Congress and outside, and their challenge to Gandhiji's last mission to establish a technique as to how people should resist the international forces of dis-integration in government and in society. Therefore, as an individual resister she carried on the activities of a Shanti Sainik in J&K State and for the people of J&K in the rest of India.

For the Users

An eminent woman who participated in the freedom struggle and worked for promoting communal harmony.

REFERENCE

Basu, Aparna, Mridula Sarabhai: *Rebel with a Cause 2003,* Oxford University Press, New Delhi.

Jaishri Raiji

Dedicated her life to social work in 1918.
Imprisoned during the Quit India Movement in 1942.
President of Bhagini Samaj, Bombay for ten years 1932-43.
Patron of the All India Women's Conference 1968.
Attended International Conference on Social Work at Toronto (Canada) 1954.

Jaishri Raiji was born in Surat in a well-to-do family. Her parents were great supporters of girls' education. It is because of their constant encouragement that she graduated from Baroda College and Bombay University. She married N.M. Raiji, a well known Chartered Accountant at Bombay, and began living there.

She dedicated her entire life to social work. As an ardent Congress worker and follower of Mahatma Gandhi, she actively participated in the freedom movement. Her participation became more visible in the Quit India Movement. Later, she was also imprisoned.

In post independent India, she took a leading part in the passage of important social legislation such as the "Hindu Code Bill" and the "Suppression of Immoral Traffic in Women and Children". She sponsored the Dowry Restraint Bill and the Indian Adoption of Children Bill. As a leading Congress worker, she organised the Congress Mahila Vibhag, Bombay and was its president for several years. She worked as the President of the Bhagini Samaj, Bombay for ten years from 1932 to 1943. She took up work for Harijan and Adivasi girls. She was the President of the Bombay Women's Council in 1929 and served on its Rescue and Parlimentary Committee. As a Fellow of the Bombay University Senate, she represented the university in the Bombay Municipal Corporation from 1939 to 1943. She was appointed as a Director to rehabilitate and give relief to displaced women after partition.

She was closely associated with All India Women's Conference and even became its Vice President. In fact, she was made a Patron of the A.I.W.C. in 1968. She has to her credit many articles on social reform. She has also travelled widely in Europe and U.S.A. She attended the International Conference of Social Work at Toranto (Canada) in 1954.

For the Users

This is an account of a woman who selflessly worked for the upliftment of women and had the distinction of participating in the struggle for independence.

REFERENCES

Cour, Ajeet and Cour, Arpana, (Ed.) (1976): *Directory of Indian Women Today,* International Publication, New Delhi.

Volume on Diamond Jubilee 1927-87, All India Women's Conference, New Delhi.

Mother Teresa

Took the name of Sister Teresa-1928.
Founded the Order of Missionaries of Charity-1950.
She got Padma Shri for her services to the people-1963.
Pope John Paul II awarded her the first Pope John XXIII Peace Prize-1971.
Awarded the Joseph Kennedy Jr. Peace Prize for the services to the mentally retarded.
Recipient of the Jawaharlal Nehru Award for International Understanding.
Won the Nobel Peace Prize-1979.
Got the Bharat Ratna-1980.

"An Apostle of peace, a walking saint who constantly worked for the upliftment of the humanity, especially the weak, the downtrodden, the sick and the neglected. Her ceaseless service for the upliftment of humanity has given her the title of Mother".

Mother Teresa dedicated her life to the service of the "poorest of the poor" as she believed that in serving the poorest, she was serving God. Her life was a story of love and compassion. To the millions of sick, abandoned poor and dying she brought help and relief.

She was born on August 27, 1910 in Albania, Yugoslavia. She was the daughter of an Albanean grocer and was earlier known as Agnes Gonxha Bojaxhin. At the age of twelve, she decided to become a nun, and at the age of eighteen, she joined the order of Loreto nuns in Ireland. On joining the order, Agnes took on the name "Teresa". There, in that distant land, she got the call to go to India. "It is a missionary country like the countries of Africa", she explained when asked why she chose India. And it was in Calcutta that she arrived in 1929, to become a teacher in Loreto School. "I love teaching most of all", she said. She devoted 17 years of her life to it.

On September 10, 1946, while on a train journey to Darjeeling, she heard the 'Voice of God' from within, asking her to leave the convent and serve the "poorest of the poor". "The message was clear", she said, "but I had to wait for the permission from the Pope to be released from Loreto Order and to start on my own".

After getting the Pope's permission, she left the school, discarded the nun's dress i.e. black and white, and wore a coarse, blue-bordered sari. She became an Indian citizen in 1948 and came to be known as Mother Teresa. She set up an organisation, the 'Missionaries of Charity'. It began formally in October, 1950.

In the initial years, Mother Teresa faced a lot of difficulties because money and help were scarce. But this did not discourage her. In her own words she said, "If he shows you a need to be served, he will provide the resource". She began her work by gathering a few children around her, picking up a stick and drawing the letters of the Bengali alphabets on the ground. Gradually, people came forward and donated a chair, blackboard and some of the teachers volunteered their services to the school.

Her services, especially towards the downtrodden, became evident when she picked a woman from the street who was half eaten by rats and ants. Her condition was so pathetic that even after nursing her she could not be saved. She breathed her last in Mother's arms. This incident saddened Mother and she resolved to give her life and soul to serve the neglected and the downtrodden. It strengthened her resolve to build a home where the abandoned could live and die with dignity. This quest led her to Kalighat in Calcutta where the Corporation gave her some empty halls. This became the first home for the dying and she called it "Nirmal Hriday". She established 62 Homes for the dying poor all over India. They are run by the Missionaries of Charity. In this Home no one has the feeling of being unwanted or unloved.

Mother Teresa's second mission of mercy was towards the poor, orphaned and abandoned children. This led her to establish the Nirmal Shishu Bhavan. Over the years, about 10,000 children have been brought up at the Bhavan. As babies they were cradled in the arms of the sisters, and as they grew up, they were schooled and trained for a profession. Later, they were helped to settle down in life. Poster for the visitors at the Bhavan clearly portrays Mother's message, "The poor want your love, not only your services. To give love you have to give a part of yourself".

Her third significant focus was for the lepers, victims of leprosy, who were usually disowned, abandoned and shunned by their families. She built "Prem Nivas", the Home of love for them. Lepers from all over India could come and join the Home. In her own words she said, "When I wash a leper's wounds, I feel I am nursing the Lord Himself". Touch a leper, touch him with love, was Mother's motto.

Mother Teresa's work gradually acquired an international status. Missionaries of Charity became a world wide congregation of thousands of sisters and brothers, priests and volunteers, drawn from various nationalities. Spread over 120 countries, the Order runs educational establishments, clinics, homes for the poor and hospital for AIDS patients. When asked about the transition of her Missionaries of Charity from a small order to a large institution, Mother retorted, "It is not an institution. It is love in action. It is the sign that it is God's work, not my work. Although we have grown so big, we are still a family".

> "I was hungry and you fed me,
> I was naked and you clothed me,
> I was sick and you visited me,
> I was homeless and you took me in,
> Whatever you did, you did it to me".

Since the poor, neglected and the sick were found throughout the world, she travelled widely, setting up islands of hope for the neglected and the poor. She had once said that she was prepared to go to the Moon, if there are poor'. Through her thoughts, words and deeds, Mother showed the world that if one has the will and the milk of human kindness', one can see God in every human being. If you judge people, you have no time to love them.

She drew her strength from the prayers and the Mass that she attended every morning. For her, the Christ on her crucifix and the one who lay abandoned on the streets were not different from each other. Hundreds and thousands of suffering human beings benefited from Mother's love and care. She would often say, "My work is just a drop when what is needed is an ocean of compassion. If I did not put in that one drop, the ocean would be one drop less."

Mother Teresa received several awards for her service to the downtrodden. Among the several awards she received was Nobel Peace Prize, the Leo Tolstoy International Award, the Bharat Ratna, the British Order of Merit, the Ceres Medal of the FAO, to put it briefly. Since the Nobel Peace Prize in 1979, she had received over 50 national and international awards. "These awards are not for me. They are for the poor who are being recognised", she said. In fact, she did not want anything for herself. She considered herself an instrument of God.

All the awards which carried cash were spent on the poor and the suffering humanity. When the former Pope Paul VI gifted her the magnificent limousine in which she travelled in India, she organised a raffle for the car and the money collected was spent on a leprosy centre. When Mother received the Pope John XXII Peace Prize in 1971, the cash award of $21,500 which it carried, went to the cause of leprosy patients. The construction of a children's Home in Agra would have been abandoned if Mother had not donated the cash prize of Rs. 50,000 which came with the Magsaysay Award.

Mother Teresa left this world on September 5, 1997, in Calcutta. As the world's most recognised symbols of compassion, hundreds of important Indians and world personalities came to pay their last homage to the "Living Saint". Tributes poured in from all over the world for one who had dedicated her entire life to the suffering humanity. The most articulate, perhaps, was by the French President

Jaquees Chirac, "This evening there is less love, less compassion, less light in the world"

For the Users

This is a poignant portrayal of an Albanian nun who made India her home and dedicated her entire life to the upliftment of the destitute and the downtrodden. Her services to humanity were recognised nationally and internationally. In fact, she became a living saint, constantly working for the good of humanity. The order founded by her also dedicated their service for the cause she stood for.

REFERENCES

Chawla, Navin, *Mother Teresa: The Authorised Biography.*

Datta, S.C., (1993): *Five Eminent Women,* Anmol Publication, New Delhi.

Sebba, Anne, Mother Teresa: Beyond the Image, Weidenfeld and Nicolson, London, 1997.

Rameshwari Nehru

President of the All India Harijan Sewak Sangh in 1935.
Founder President of the Delhi Women's League in 1926.
Editor of the Magazine "Stree Darpan" 1909.
Took active part in the Swadeshi and Independence Movement in 1942.
Awarded the Lenin Prize in 1951.
Awarded Padma Bhushan in 1955.

Smt. Rameshwari Nehru, an outstanding social worker, was born in 1886 in Lahore.

She devoted a great part of her time and energy, under Gandhi's inspiration, to the upliftment of Harijans. She was President of the All India Harijan Sewak Sangh from 1935 onwards. Throughout her life she strove to eliminate completely the curse of untouchability.

She was the founder and President of Delhi Women's League in 1926 (Delhi Branch of the A.I.W.C. and worked for abolition of child marriage and caste prejudices and for the spread of Education. Also, she was the editor of the magazine "Stree Darpan" and one of the organisers of the Afro-Asian Conference.

REFERENCE

All India Women's Conference, Diamond Jubilee 1927-87, Sarojini House, 6 Bhagwan Dass Road, New Delhi.

Sarojini Varadappan

Secretary of the Women's Indian Association–1953.
Member of the Madras State Social Welfare Board–1954.
General Secretary of All India Women's Conference–1959-61.
President of A.I.W.C. from 1980 to 1985.
Studied the problems of deck passengers at Singapore and Penang in 1956.

Sarojini Varadappan was born at Madras. She was the daughter of Bhakthavatsalam, a leading patriot of Tamil Nadu who later served as a Minister. From a very young age she was closely connected with the welfare of women and the downtrodden. She started her public career as a Congress Seva Dal volunteer and since 1953 she was the Secretary of the Women's Indian Association. She also served as a member of the Madras State Social Welfare Board since its inception in 1954. She, later on, became the chairperson of the Central Social Welfare Board.

From 1959 to 1961, she served A.I.W.C. as its General Secretary. Also, she had been its Vice President and later President from 1980 to 1985.

When she was connected with Women's Welfare Department, she had the opportunity to come in contact with various women's groups and study their needs. She held various positions in different committees and commissions. She served as a Treasurer of the Madras State Food Council; Member of the Management Committee, Victoria Technical Institute; Member of the Special Welfare Panel in Planning Commission. Also, she had been member of the Madras University Senate, Madras All India Radio, Bharat Scouts and Nehru Fund, Jawaharlal Nehru Fund, Kasturba National

Memorial Trust; National Council for Women. She had been the President of Tamil Nadu Council for Air Force Welfare and President of Women's Consumer Cooperative; and Hony. Magistrate of Juvenile Court for 15 years. She had travelled extensively all over the world. In 1958, she visited Europe and in 1964 she visited U.S.A. She also visited Japan. Hongkong, Bangkok, Ceylon. In 1956 she went to Singapore and Penang to study the problems of deck passengers. She represented India at the U.N. Conference on 'Status of Women at Manila.

For the Users

This is the story of a woman who firmly believed that service to humanity was service to god. She not only worked selflessly for her fellow beings but held numerous responsible positions in Government organisations. She travelled widely and represented India internationally.

REFERENCES

Cour, Ajeet and Cour, Arpana, (Ed.) (1976): *Directory of Indian Women Today,* International Publications, New Delhi.

Volume on Diamond Jubilee 1927-87, All India Women's Conference, New Delhi.

Renuka Ray

Joined the London School of Economics in 1921.
Presided over All India Women's Conference in 1932.
Nominated to the Central Assembly to represent women's organisations and fought for women's right in 1943.
Minister, Relief and Rehabilitation, West Bengal in 1952-57.
Member, Lok Sabha, in 1957-67.
Delegate to the Inter-Parliamentary Union in 1966-67.
President of All India Women's Conference in 1953-54.

Renuka Ray was born in 1904 in a well-to-do family. She was the daughter of Satishchandra Mukherji (I.C.S.) and Charulata Mukherji. Renuka was the eldest of four children. While she was studying in Diocesan Girl's College in Calcutta, she met Mahatma Gandhi. His appeal for non cooperation moved her tremendously and she decided to give up her studies and join the movement. Her parents, however, asked Gandhiji to persuade her to go to England to study.

Renuka joined the London School of Economics in 1921 and was a student of Harold Laski. In England, she met S.N. Ray, who was then studying at King's College, Cambridge and later joined the I.C.S.

On her return to India, Renuka became deeply concerned with the lot of women. She founded Mahila Samitis in the district of Bengal where her husband was posted. She also started the branches of All India Women's Conference in the district. In fact, Gandhiji asked her to concentrate on rural reconstruction work.

She later on presided over the All India Women's Conference in 1932. Further, when the A.I.W.C. undertook a campaign for a uniform civil code she took an active part along with other women vigorously campaigning and mobilising support. In 1943, she was nominated to the Central Assembly to represent women's organisation and fought for women's right.

She was a member of the Constituent Assembly and Provisional Parliament, Minister, Relief and Rehabilitation, West Bengal, 1952-57, Member, Lok Sabha, 1957-67. She was a delegate to the Inter Parliamentary Union, 1966-77. She was the President of All India Women's Conference, 1953-54 and represented A.I.W.C. in various international forums and was a delegate to the U.N. General Assembly.

She wrote several articles and pamphlets and her autobiography *My Reminiscences* was a mirror of her times.

Throughout her life, she was deeply concerned with the socio-economic development of the country as a whole and particularly the status of women.

For the Users

The noted social worker worked relentlessly for raising the status of girls and women and campaigned for a uniform civil code. She held various political positions in West Bengal and in the centre.

REFERENCES

Volume on Diamond Jubilee, 1927-87, All India Women's Conference, New Delhi.

Basu, Aparna, "Renuka Ray (1904-1997)": *Roshini,* Journal of A.I.W.C., July 1997, New Delhi.

Amrita Pritam

Awarded Sahitya Akademi Award in 1956.
Honoured with Padmashri in 1969.
Got the Jnanpith Award in 1981.

Foremost Punjabi poetess Amrita Pritam was born in Gujranwala (now in Pakistan) on 31st August, 1919. She was the only child of a school teacher and poet. She lost her mother at a very young age of eleven. This tragic incident had a deep impact on her personal life. Her father was a great source of encouragement but was not very happy with the theme she selected for her poems and other forms of literary expressions. She began to write at an early age, and her first collection was published when she was only 16 years old, the year she married an editor to whom she was engaged in early childhood. Destiny took a turn when partition took place. The family had to migrate to India (Delhi) from Lahore.

Her literary career for the last almost half a century is largely related to the literary history of the Punjabi language during the period. She ushered in a new era of the Punjabi literary movement. Her contribution to the enrichment of the various of modern literary forms—poetry, novel short story, autobiographical and literary essays in remarkable. All these reflect the human predicament particularly as seen through the eyes of a woman, an agony and the ecstasy which haunts. Her poem Waris Shah is a remarkable testament of the anguish of the violated women. Her poems are full of humour, evocative imagery and restrained passion which could easily pass for classical excellence.

A prolific writer she has published more than 75 books. She has bagged a number of literary awards including Sahitya Akademi Award in 1956 for her book of poems Sunehra and the Jnanpith

Award in 1981 for her collection of poems Kagaj te Kanvas. Her literary works have been translated into a number of Indian and foreign languages such as English, Albania, Bulgarian, French, Polish, Russian, Spanish and all the 21 Indian languages. She has published 75 books of which—28 are novels, 18 volumes of verse, five short stories and 16 miscellaneous prose. Besides this, she also edited the Punjab literary journal "Nagmani". Two of her novels Dharti Sagar te Sippiyan (1965) and Unah Di Kahani (1976) have been made into films titled "Kadambari" and "Daaku" for which she even composed songs.

Amrita was deeply influenced by the problem and trials of common men and women. Some of her writings touch up on these issues.

Few of her well read poems are Kastrui (Music) and Nagamani (Serpent's Jewel) published in 1959 and 1964 respectively. Her short stories remain a class apart. Some of her well known short stories are — *Shekar De Maut, Tessari Aurat* and *Panj Vareh Lambi Sarak.* Her autobiography Rashidi Tickat. (The Revenue Stamp) was first published in Punjabi in 1976. She was also nominated as a Member of the Rajya Sabha. Amrita Pritan will always live and breathe through her works. In 2003, her Partition classic 'Pinjar' was filmed into a critically acclaimed movie by the same name.

She was conferred D. Litt. (Honorary by Viswa Bharti, Delhi, Jabalpur and Punjab Universities). She was also conferred degree of "Officer dans/order des arts et. Des Letters" by French Government.

For the Users

The Punjabi poetess through her pen depicted various facets of human emotions and won various literary awards for her contributions and also the nation's highest civilian award.

REFERENCES

Jain, C.K. (1993): *Women Parliamentarians in India,* Surjeet Publication, New Delhi.

An Album of Indian Writers; Issues on the occasion of Frankfurt World Book Fair, 1986, Sahitya Akademi, (National Academy of Letters), New Delhi.

The Times of India, New Delhi, November 1, 2005.

Ashapurna Devi

Release of her Publication Jal Aar Agun—a short story collection in 1940.
Published a novel Prem O Prayojan in 1944.
Awarded Jnanpith Award in 1976.
Honoured with Padma Shree in 1976.

Ashapurna Devi was born on January 8, 1909. Brought up in a conservative middle class family, she had little opportunity to go in for formal education. But being an avid reader of Bengali literature, she pursued her studies at home. Since the release of her first publication in 1940, *Jal Aar Agun,* a short story collection, and *Prem O Prayojan*—a novel in 1944, she took giant leaps in the field of Bengali literature.

She is the recipient of a number of literary awards including Leela Award and Rabindra Award. She bagged the prestigious Jnanpith Award for her epic novel *Pratham Pratishurti* in 1976. She was also honoured with 'Padma Shree, in 1976.

She is best known for her famous trilogy *Pratham Pratishruti, Subarnalata* and *Babul Katha* which depict her revolt against worn out social customs and conventions of Bengal. These novels established her as a rebel writer fighting against the indignity of women. She continues to be a popular writer among the middle class and especially among women readers.

A number of her novels and short stories have been translated into other Indian languages and in English. In fact, with six decades of creative pursuit behind her, she has become a legend of modern Bengali literature. Her 135 novels, 23 short collections and 22 children books constitute some of the finest literary pieces in India today.

For the Users

A novelist and a short story writer who left her mark in the field of Bengali language and literature. She is the winner of several prestigious awards and also the highest civilian award of the nation.

REFERENCE

An Album of Indian Writers; Issued on the occasion of Frankfurt World Book Fair, 1986, Sahitya Akademi, (National Academy of Letters), New Delhi.

Amrita Shergil

Painting entitled "A Group of Young Girls", which is painted at Amritsar secured her a gold medal at the Bombay Art Exhibition in 1935.

Awarded a gold medal and the Chief Commissioner's Prize for the best portrait at the Delhi exhibition in 1936.

Earned distinction and medals in all exhibitions in all art centres of India in 1938.

Amrita Shergil was born in Budapest, Hungary in 1913. Her father Sardar Umroo Singh Shergil was an Indian and a man who had tremendous aesthetic sense. Her mother Marie Antoinette was a Hungarian lady who was a gifted singer and a musician and possessed great artistic talent.

Amrita was brought up in the beautiful surrounding of Hungary and the first language spoken by her was Hungarian. Since her childhood days Amrita was a gifted artist. She could draw all the toys around her very accurately. In the words of her mother, "It was remarkable how well she could copy all the toys around her—dolls, carts and teddy bear". In her own words she stated that:

"I have drawn and painted, I think, from my tiniest childhood, and I recollect that the presents I most looked forward to as a child were paint boxes, colour pencils, drawing-papers, and picture books. Rather independent in spirit even at that age, it will be of psychological interest to note that I detested the process of 'colouring in' the drawing's of picture books and never allowed 'grown-ups' to draw things for me to colour in (a practice that most children adore, leaving the most difficult task, drawing, to others and monopolising the more natural and pleasant one of colours for themselves). I always drew and painted everything myself and resented correction or interference with my work". Her childhood playmate and first cousin, Victor Egan, whom she eventually married, had known her since the day she was born. He, too, remembers that even as a little child—

"She showed signs of becoming an artist because, in an amusingly childish way, she would draw or paint on any bit of paper she could find, even on a torn envelop or any scrap of paper she could lay her hands on. She would paint on the wall. The house used to be littered with her drawings. She was never interested in a black pencil; it had to be coloured. The pictures she often drew were of funny looking creatures, some looking like human beings".

Even before seven, she was able to illustrate little stories told to her by her parents. Later on, she could compose her own fairy stories, illustrating them with coloured crayons. Her parents engaged a qualified university student to acquaint Amrita and her sister with the knowledge of 3R's (i.e.reading writing and arithmetics). Her intellingence was clearly revealed when she mastered reading, writing and arithmetic quickly and also made remarkable improvements on them. She was very fond of history and developed her favourite pass time of recording events with coloured crayons and water colours.

In 1921 when the freedom struggle in India had acquired a mass base particularly under the leadership of Mahatma Gandhi and with the non cooperation movement going on, Amrita Shegil along with her parents came to India. They settled at Shimla.

Amrita's education in India progressed at the Jesus and Mary Convent. Her father engaged a teacher to give her and her sister lessons in English. In fact, with the help of good teachers, they were able to express themselves fluently. Regular class work developed Amrita's remarkable good memory and , in particular, her love for drawing and painting. Bevan Petman, who was Amrita's teacher, was extremely impressed by her. In his own words he stated that, "I opened my heart to her (Marie Antoinette) and told her that in my opinion Amrita was possessed of a rare talent that should be carefully nurtured and encouraged, and that I felt she had all the making of a brilliant artist". He suggested to her parents that they should take her to Europe. A teacher was also engaged to give Amrita and her sister lessons in drawing and violin. The teacher commented at the end of the first month on Amrita's unusual ability and quick response. He would tell stories of his own fancy and she would immediately draw pictures through her imagination.

Her keen interest in drawing and painting made her parents decide to go to France which was considered during the 20th century as one of the great centres of art in the world. The "Young Girls" had won her associateship of the Grand Salon, the critics in Paris had also taken notice of this particular picture. It was at the instance of Mr. Nemes, who was a Hungarian painter friend of Amrita's family and also a greater admirer of her work, that she was introduced to Professor Lucien Simon of the Ecole National des Beaux Arts. The Professor was extremely impressed by Amrita's painting and despite her age (she was under eighteen years and was not eligible for admission). She was given admission in this famous school of Art.

The constant encouragement she got from Professor Simon, proved a blessing in disguise. It was at this centre that she painted the famous "Young Girls"—then titled "Conversation" which won her the much conveted distinction of Associate at the Grand Salon of 1930. A big party was arranged by the Professor to felicitate her achievement. Amrita continued to work deligently at the Beaux Art where she achieved more distinction. She was awarded first prize for still life compositions and also a gold medal for her self-portrait.

During the years 1930-32, she painted several pictures, mostly in oils and they were portraits on portrait studies, barring a couple of landscapes done in Hungary.

The year 1933 was a memorable year in Amrita's life. It was the year she achieved the distinction of becoming an Associate of the Grand Salon.

By 1934, Amrita had reached an advanced stage and she suddenly had a desire to return to India. Though her professor was very sad in loosing his good student he said that for his talented pupil, her art and powerful sense of colour would have great scope for expression in India than in the dull grey atmosphere of the Paris studios. Settled once again in India, Amrita soon readapted herself to her surrounding. At the end of two months she had already painted an excellent picture in Amritsar titled "A Group of Young Girls" which eventually secured her the first prize and also a gold medal at the Bomaby Art Exhibition in 1935. The same year she refused the prize awarded to her at the Simla Fine Arts Exhibition for strong reasons of her own.

She worked deligently at her studio at Simla. Most of the paintings done at this studio received prominent mention in the French art journals. In India, there was a gradual change in her style of painting. She adopted Indian dresses, environment, particularly the saree was constantly used in her portrait drawing.

At the exhibition held in 1936 at Delhi, she was awarded a gold medal and the Chief Commissioner's Prize for the best portrait. In fact, this was the same painting that brought her the first gold medal in Paris. The Times of India, which was then, and still is, the leading daily in Bombay, described Amrita Shergil as one of the most promising of the younger generation of Indian painters".

The exhibition of her paintings followed till 1938 in all the art centres of India where she attained various distinctions and gold medals.

In 1938, Amrita broke all conventions by marrying her cousin Mr. Victor Egan.

In fact, Amrita's contribution to painting clearly depicts her symbolic relation to the art and culture of her age. Her greatest ambition was to study, to learn, to observe correctly and to create something noble, permanent and significant. She was also a great scholar of art and literature, and would never read a book which did not powerfully impress her imagination. Her four major interest of her fancy were mythology, history, romance and poetry.

Her last three pictures titled, "The Camels," "Elephant Head" and "The Basket Weavers" painted at Saraya, U.P. in 1941 within a short span of less than a month depicts her great step towards perfection in art, with regards to colour, design and composition.

There is a consensus among the art historians and critics about the divergence in Amrita's painting done in Hungary and the paintings executed in India. They are "Entirely European in their colour, mood and sensibility."

Most of her paintings are kept at the National Gallery of Modern Art, New Delhi or possessed by private persons. The distribution of her paintings is as follows:

1. National Gallery of Modern Art, New Delhi

1. Girls in Field, 1932
2. Boat, 1934
3. Klara Szepess Y, 1934
4. My Grandmother, 1934
5. The Potato Peeler, 1938
6. Hungarian Market Scene, 1938
7. Nude, 1938
8. Hungarian Peasant, 1939
9. The Merry Cemetery, 1939
10. Winter, 1939

II. Mr. Sundaram, New Delhi

1. Hungarian Village Church, 1932
2. Hungarian Church Steeple, 1938
3. Two Girls, 1939

III. Mrs. Erno Gottesmann, Budapest

1. Gipsy Girls from Zebegeny, 1932
2. Portrait of Victor Egan, 1932
3. Portrait of Mrs. Erno Gottesmann, Viola Egan, 1934
4. Self Portriat, 1932

IV. D.S. Majithia

1. Hungarian Market Scene

V. Dr. Victor Egan (Sardar Nagar, Distt. Gorakhpur)

1. Portrait of Victor Egan in Military Uniform, 1938

In fact, Amrita Shergil's contribution to the field of art was a synthesis of her rich Hungarian experiences, the Indian traditions and the demands of modern painting. In seven brief years of pictorial activity, she left behind, after her tragic death, a name that is gratefully remembered by all who love beauty and creative art.

For the Users

This is the story of a god gifted painter who painted in her canvas the common sight and surroundings in which she grew. Her work is a beautiful blend of European and Indian motifs. It is through her paintings that she attained an international position of eminence in the field of art.

REFERENCES

Dandavate, Madhu (1989): *Architects of Modern India,* Published by V.N.O. Key Felicitation Committee, Bombay.

Wojtilla, Gyula (1981): *Amrita Shergil and Hungary,* Allied Publishers Private Limited, New Delhi.

Mrinalini Sarabhai

Founded the Darpana Akademi in Ahmedabad in 1948.
Won the Sangeet Natak Akademi Award in 1970.
D. Litt. from Rabindra Bharati University, Calcutta in 1979.
Awarded Desikottam from Viswa Bharti in 1987.
Watumull Prize from Hawai in 1987.

Mrinalini Sarabhai was born on 7th May, 1928 in Madras. Her father Dr. G. Swaminathan was a barrister-at-law; her mother Ammu Swaminathan was a widely known social worker and Member of Parliament.

She took to dancing at the tender age of five. In fact, she became a disciple of K. (Kattumannarkoil) Muthukumara Pillai who was teaching Bharatanatyam in Kalakshetra, Adayar (Madras). Latter on, he became a guru in Mrinalini's own Darpana Akademi founded in 1948. Her husband Dr. Vikram Sarabhai, a brilliant scientist, gave tremendous support to her dance career. In 1949, soon after her marriage she received an invitation for a one hour recital in Paris. Her performance was highly appreciated and she hit the headlines in most of the leading newspapers.

It was under Dr. Sarabhai's inspiration that the now internationally renowned "Darpana Akademi of Performing Art" was founded in Ahmedabad in 1948. Initially Bharatanatyam, Kuchipudi, Kathakali and Mohiniattam were taught by a team of expert gurus. Subsequently she added another discipline into Darpana—the leather. Shadow puppets of Indonesian Ramayana and the traditional leather - puppets of Andhra Pardesh inspired her to start a department of puppetry. The backbone of Darpana is Bharatanatyam.

Mrinalini and her Darpana troupe have performed abroad more than 25 times since 1949, and have performed in over 40 countries covering all the major cities of Europe, U.S.A., U.S.S.R., Middle East, China, Japan, South-East Asia and North, Central and South America. Her book "Creation gives a complete list of dance creations chronologically.

Among her many collaborative productions with Western world was the Sanskrit play Swapna Vasvadatta in which Mrinalini directed American actors for the New York Institute of Advanced Studies in Theatre Art in 1963. The play was entitled "The Vision of Vasavadatta". In 1970, she, alongwith Milorad Miskovitch and Carla Fracci, performed in a ballet of Beethoven called, "The Creatures of Prometheus" during the bicentenary celebration of this great composer. This ballet was presented in many cities in Italy and won much acclaim. As a tribute to Franz Schubert, Mrinalini presented "Shakuntala" based on a rare manuscript of Schubert's in Vienna.

Creations truly reflects her philosophy, aesthetics, her wide ranging interests, her concern for harmony between man and nature, and for the oppressed—all of which she expressed in her language of dance.

For her contributions to the art, Mrinalini has won innumerable awards and titles such as Natya Kala-Sikhamani from Madras, Sangeet Natak Akademi award in 1970, D. Litt. from the Rabindra Bharati University, Calcutta in 1979, Desikottama from Viswa Bharti in 1987, Veera Srinkhala for her Kathakali, an honorary Doctorate from Viswa Bharati, the Watumull Prize from Hawai in 1987 and many medals from Paris, Mexico and so on.

Hailed as "the Martha Graham of India", Mrinalini has taken Indian dancing all over the world in its classical purity, and in the spirit of India's contemporary vision.

For the Users

This is the story of a Gujarati woman who raised the classical dance of India to an international stage and won several prestigious national and international awards for it. She is also a founder member of an internationally renowned academy

REFERENCE

Misra, Susheela (1972); *Some Dancers of India.* New Delhi.

Sanjukta Panigrahi

First Presentation of Odissi dance at the age of eight at the International Children Festival in Calcutta in 1953.
Won a Scholarship from Government of Orissa to undergo a training at Kalakshetra, Madras in 1954.
Awarded 'Nritya Praveena' in Bharatanatyam in 1958.
Honoured with Padma Shri in 1975.

Sanjukta Panigrahi was born in 1944 in a respectable well-to-do orthodox Brahmin family. From early childhood she was keenly interested in dancing. Her father was opposed to her interest in dance and firmly believed that no girl from a respectable family should take to it. However, her mother encouraged her and at a tender age of four Sanjukta was placed under the tutelage of Guru Kelucharan Mohapatra.

Her first dance performance was at the age of eight. She presented an Odissi recital at the International Children's Festival in Calcutta in 1953. In fact, her performance was so good that she charmed the crowd, connoisseur and critics alike.

It was her charm that enthralled the audience for the next forty years and more. She never looked back as she went on performing all over the country. She won a scholarship in 1954 from the Government of Orissa, the first of its kind, to undergo training at Kalakshetra, Madras, under Rukmani Devi Arundale.

For her excellent performance and contributon to dance she was awareded 'Nritya Praveena' in Bharatanatyam four years later. Meanwhile, she had also kept up her Odissi training and was awarded the diploma of 'Nrityashree' by the Kala Vikas Kendra, Cuttack.

Her decision to commit herself heart and soul to Odissi dance was because of constant support and encouragement provided by her husband, the well known and melodious, 'Gita Govind' singer Raghunath Panigrahi. Later, she was amply rewarded when it became a popular form of classical dance in the national and international arena. Her flawless execution of mudras, superb synchronization of movements and impeccable footwork, apart from her excellent mimetic process, made her one of the finest classical dancers that India has ever produced.

She won several honours including the Padma Shree in 1975; toured extensively all over the world; served as the country's cultural delegate to many countries; was even awarded honorary citizenship of cities abroad. Her tour of Australia in July, 1996 was her last.

Apart from her undeniable versatility as a dancer, she ceaselessly enriched the dance form that made her a complete artist, who had few equals. In close collaboration with other scholars, she devoted her time to the study of ancient Odissi literature, palm leaf inscriptions, temple figures, temple dancers of 'Maharis' and 'Goptipua' with a view to codifying the nomenclature of the Odissi style.

For the Users

This is a portrayal of a famous Odissi dancer whose performance won her national and international fame. She was recipient of both national and international awards.

REFERENCES

Singh, Shanta Serbjeet, "The Eternal Shishya", *The Hindustan Times, 5 July*, 1997, New Delhi.

Mishra, Bibhuti, "Sanjukta Elevated and Enriched Odissi", *The Indian Express,* 25 June, 1997, New Delhi.

Mishra, Susheela, *Some Dancers of India,* New Delhi. 1972.

Upadhyay, Madhu, *Profiles in Creativity, Printed at Sri Sudhindra* Offset Process, Banglaore, 1990.

M.S. Subbulakshmi

Most memorable performance was Bhaktha Meera in Meera–1945
Gave remarkable concert at Carnegie Hall, New York and U.N. General Assembly–1966
Awarded Padma Vibhushan–1975
Got the Padma Bhushan–1954
Ramon Magsaysay Award–1974
Kalidas Samman–1998
Received the Bharat Ratna–1996

The legendary Carnatic vocalist, Ms. M.S. Subbulakshmi had few parallels. She had immensely contributed to enrich the classical musical heritage of India. Singing to the world at large for over five decades, she became a symbol of all pervading versatility.

M.S. Subbulakshmi (popularly known as MS) was born on September 16, 1916, to Madurai Shanmukhav Adiver Ammal and Subramania Iyer in the temple town of Madurai in Tamil Nadu. MS had studied up to class 5 and had to discontinue studies owing to illness. Even though she had to discontinue her studies she took up another field i.e. music in which she excelled. She started learning music at a young age, especially carnatic music. She was a student of late Semmangudi Srinivasa Iyer who trained her in Carnatic music. Later, she acquired training in Hindustani classical music under Pandit Narayan Rao Vyas. At the very tender age of 10 she cut her first disc.

Her home environment was extremely conducive for promoting her talent. Her mother Shanmukhavadivu was an efficient Veena player and had also given concerts. Great musicians like Karaikudi Sambasiva Iyer, Mazhavarayanendal Subbarama Bhagavatar and Ariyakudi Ramaniya Iyengar and many instrumentalists would visit her house. They used to discuss for hours music with her mother Shanmukhavadivu. The domestic environment had a profound influence on Kunjanma (pet name). Her exposure to classical music further aroused her quest for it. At 17, she made her debut in the world of music at the Madras Music Academy. Since then, she performed in countless functions. MS was also a recipient of the highest award of the country 'Bharat Ratna' in 1996.

During her long career as a singer, MS had scaled many peaks but the Mela-raga-malika of Maha Vaidyanatha Sivam recorded by her in a single long playing record shows the perfection she had attained. Her soulful rendering of devotional music, notably Meera bhajans, are very popular.

Her records and cassettes on Meera bhajans and the 'Suprabhatam' devoted to Lord Venkteshwara have sold thousands of copies the world over.

Her husband Mr. Sadasivam was a constant source of inspiration. She was also a producer emeritus. Her first role in film which deserves special mention is Seva Sadanam (1938) followed by her superb performance in Shakuntala and Meera.

For her contribution to Indian music, M.S. Subbulakshmi was conferred various awards including the Padma Bhushan (1954), the Ramon Magsaysay Award (1974), Padma Vibhushan (1975), Isai Vani, Sangeetha Kalanidhi, Spirit of Freedom Award, and the Indira Gandhi Award for National Integration. She was awarded the highest civilian award i.e. the Bharat Ratna in 1996. In fact, she became the first musician to get this coveted honour.

In a career spanning over six decades, she had sung before great personages like Mahatma Gandhi and had given concerts at almost all the leading festivals the world over, including the well known Edinburgh Festival in Scotland and the United Nations in 1966.

A disciple of the sage of Kanchi, M.S. says, "Indian music is oriented solely to the end of divine communication. If I have done something in this respect, it is entirely due to the grace of the Almighty Who has chosen me as a humble tool in a way I take him to have come within my reach in the benign form of the sage of Kanchi".

M.S. began withdrawing from public concerts from the 1980s, performing only for exceptional causes. She stopped singing after the demise of her husband in 1997. For an artist of world acclaim, M.S. never gave a single interview, letting her music speak for itself. But she received unprecedented press coverage.

M.S. is an inspiring role model, not only for her music but also for her rare qualities of humility, compassion and principles of conduct and discipline. Between 1944 and 1987, she according to records, gave 244 charity concerts, sometimes 16 in a year. The latest such donation was the Lifetime Achievement Award money of 11 lakhs given by the Delhi Government.

This legendary musical exponent breathed her last on December 11, 2004. President A.P.J. Abdul Kalam, who led the nation in paying homage to M.S., flew down to Chennai to pay his last respect. He said, "We have lost an incomparable music exponent of our time. Her singing spread divine happiness and peace to millions of hearts arount the world".

For the Users

This is the story of the legendary Carnatic vocalist whose contribution to Indian music has been immense and which has made her the giant in her field. She won several prestigious awards including India's highest civilian award, the Bharat Ratna.

REFERENCES

Bhavans Journal, Vol. 35, No. 21, June 15, 1989, Bombay.

Upadhyay, Madhu, *Profile in Creativity,* DTP and Printed at Sri Sudhindra Offset Process, Bangalore.

Excerpted from Past Forward, as told to Gouri Ramnarayan, Oxford University Press, 1997.

Frontline, Dec. 31, 2004.

Lata Mangeshkar

Awarded Padma Bhushan in 1969.
Dada Saheb Phalke Award in 1989.
Bharat Ratna in 1996.
Zee Cine Award in 1998.

Lata Mangeshkar was born on September 28, 1929 in Indore. Her father, Dinanath Mangeshkar came from Mangeshi in Goa. He was a classical singer trained in the colourful Punjabi school of Baba Mushelkar. Having a humble beginning, he was unable to arrange proper schooling for his children. He, therefore, sought to encourage his children to take up music. This was how Lata got the foundation of musical propensities.

The meagre income of the family and later her father's death in 1942 compelled her to look for a profession. At the tender age of 13, she had to act and sing in "Pahili Manglagaur" a Marathi film by Master Vinayak Rao, father of Nanda, the well known actress.

In Pahili, Lata played the heroine's sister and sang three songs. In her own words she said that, "that day I went to work in Master Vinayak's film, there was nothing to eat in the house." She says Vinayak was happy with her performance in Pahili, and signed her as a staff artist on a monthly salary of Rs. 60. It became Rs. 350 by the time Vinayak died in 1947. Gradually his Prafull Pictures closed down. In 1945, the company shifted its headquarters to Mumbai, and Lata moved out into the big city of her dreams.

The first significant event for Lata in Mumbai was introduction to Aman Ali Khan Bhindi Bazarwala, a classical singer who accepted her as a disciple. But in the wake of partition he left India for Pakistan. Lata had to find a new guru. She found Amanat Ali, an accomplished singer. However, his death in 1951 ended her apprenticeship in classical music. She sang for a film called Majboor for the heroine. She was introduced to Master Ghulam Haidar, a close friend of Amanat Ali and a leading music director in those days. He was struck by the range and sweetness of her voice and she sang the same song she sung in Majboor later. The recording for Majboor was not easy. The song was recorded at the 32nd take. A number of music directors were present at the rehearsal room of Bombay Talkies. The first of them to come forward with an offer was Naushad, the Lucknow born music director whose melodies were largely responsible for the success of the musical films in the 50's. He signed Lata for Andaaz, a smashing box office success. Music director Bhagat Ram got her to sing for Badi Bahen. This was followed by Barsaat where Lata sang "Jiya Bekrar Hai", a song whose popularity is undiminished even today. From then on, there was no looking back.

Lata became a popular playback singer. But life was very hard for her. She had to go from studio to studio at inconvenient hours. In 1948, her song, "Piya milne ko aa, main to jeeti hoon tere bharose," became a hit. But her subsequent song "Bedard teri yaad ko seene se laga ke, rolege tassveer main tujhe paas bulake" for the film Padmini put the final seal of approval by Haider on her career. Her disciplinarian father had inculcated in her the qualities of preservance and perfection through constant practice. All this stood her in good stead throughout her life.

The film industry during those days was virtually dominated by Urdu writers and lyricists. This motivated Lata to brush up her linguistic skills. She took lessons from a maulvi (Urdu teacher) and perfected her pronunciation in Urdu as she now has over a lot of other languages, including Bengali. An unusual turn of event in 1949 dramatically thrust her career centrestage. Three big films by three major companies found simultaneous release and Lata became a household name. Bombay Talkies, Mahal, which had music by the famous master, Khemchand Prakash immortalised both the song and singer. The echoes of "Ayega, Ayega, Ayega .....Ayega Aane Wala, Ayega Ayega ..... became a classic. This continues to remain popular even to this day. Though Lata had been noticed in other

Hindi films, like Majboor, and had already sung over a 100 songs, it was this song that set her apart giving her that distinctive singing identity that was to dominate the next decade. With the release of Andaaz, which had music by Naushad, and Raj Kapoor's Barsaat, for which Shankar Jaikishan gave the music, Lata's genius found the permanent niche in the world of playback singing.

Lata has been the dominant female voice in Hindi films for over five decades now. In 1959, The times Magazine described her as the "indisputable and indispensable queen of Indian playback singers".

What distinguished Lata from other singers of her generation was the sweetness and emotional intensity of her songs. One remembers that Jawaharlal Nehru was moved to tears when she sang Pradeep's lyric "Aei Mere Watan Ke Logon" after the Chinese aggression in 1962.

Lata was the inspiration for Raj Kapoor's film Satyam Shivam Sudram. The film had nothing to fall back upon than the sheer beauty of Lata's sonorous voice. Naushad is certain that there cannot be another Lata.

By the early 1970's, Lata had a record number of songs and recording to her credit, according to the Guinness Book of Records. In fact, the Guinness Book of World Records, records her as the World's most prolific singer with over 25,000 songs to her credit. Lata is a living legend, an an icon of icons. It seems doubtful if any person has matched her output. It is said that she has sung 300 songs on an average in each of the first five years of her career and 500 songs annually during the next 23 years. Since 1974, she has managed almost 150 songs in a year. Then there are some songs in her private records. She seems to have ousted her closest rival, the late Mohammed Rafi.

Lata also sang outside films. She sang Ghalib's Ghazals for Khayyam and the saint-poet Meera's compositions. She rendered the Bhagavad Gita in her mellifluous style, giving the euphonic Sanskrit phrases a touch of eternal beauty. Devotional songs, such as bhav geet, Ganapati aartis, Jnaneshwari slokas of Sant

Jnaneshwar, the poet saint of Maharashtra, Shabads (Sikh devotional songs) and so on are parts of her extraordinary repertoire.

Lata's magnanimity of mind towards other singers of her generation is evident from her songs in Shraddhanjali, the cassette album of her songs released by the Gramophone Company of India on September 30, 1992 where she pays singular tribute to six of the masters who influenced and enriched her own music—K.L. Sehgal, Pankaj Mullick, Mohammad Rafi, Mukesh, Hemant Kumar and Kishore Kumar.

Lata Mangeshkar has completed over 60 years in the music industry and her voice has enthralled generations of Indians not only in India but also all over the world. It is believed by critics that she has been the most popular singer in the world exceeding 8,000 recordings. She has the world record of having sung in almost 20 languages for over 1,825 films and has worked with 165 composers.

Recipient of Padma Bhushan in 1969 and Dada Saheb Phalke Award in 1989, Lata has been widely acclaimed by her contemporaries.

Lata sang for Nargis, Madhubala and Nutan in the 1950s. She sang for Sadhana, Asha Parekh and Sharmila Tagore in the 1960's, for Zeenat Aman, Jaya Bhaduri in 1970's and for Zeba Bakhtiar in the 1990's. The stars aged, retired and faded, but Lata sang on, almost like an unperturbed immortal. The melody queen has been singing since the age of 13.

"I wear my music the way Karna wore his Kavach", said Lata Mangeshkar, the Indian nightingale at her golden jubilee felicitation function at Mumbai on September 28, 1992. In fact, she has infused life into the unending streams of songs in her inimitable voice.

The poet writer Javed Akhtar has said about her that, "The earth has but one sun, one moon and one Lata". Lata is infinity.

For the Users

The nightingale of India, started singing at a very tender age and her melodious voice held the audience in rapture. Her contribution to music has made her win several awards nationally and internationally.

REFERENCES

Ahuja, M.L., *Glimpses of Some Great Indians,* Vikas Publishing House, New Delhi, 1997

Bhavan's Journal, 31, August 2004, Vol. 5, No. 2, Bharatiya Vidya Bhawan, Mumbai.

Meena Kumari

Shot into stardom with the release of Baiju Bawra-1952
Her greatest performance was in Pakeezah-1971

Meena Kumari ruled the Hindi cinema through the 1950s and 60s. She was a legend in her lifetime and continues to be a source of inspiration to all women even in contemporary times. Her father Ali Bux was a theatre actor, singer and a music teacher and her mother Iqbal Begum was a dancer. She was born in Bombay in 1933. Her pen-name was Naaz. She wrote poems in Urdu under this name. At the tender age of six she acted in her first film. She rose to stardom in the early fifties with the release of Baiju Bawra (1952). Earlier, she was known as Mahajabeen and took the name of Meena Kumari from Vijay Bhatt's immensely popular musical film Baiju Bawra.

Some of her memorable movies that earned her fame were—"Daera", Do Bigha Zameen, Parineeta. In fact, Parineeta (1953) became a turning point in her career. Her portrayal was that of a perennially suffering Indian woman. For most of the people she was the "tragedy queen". Beside the above mentioned films, the roles that brought her fame were in Guru Dutt's—Sahib Bini Aur Ghulam (1962), Ek hi Raasta (1965) and Sharda (1957). Her last performance was in Pakeezah (1971), which was jointly conceived with her husband Kamal Amrohi. This film was completed shortly before her tragic death in 1972. In fact, Pakeezah remains till date one of the greatest Hindi films to capture the ambience and essence of Awadhi culture. The film was a super hit. Her emotional traumas and her heavy addiction to alcohol had a negative impact on her health. Life took its toll on this incredibly talented actress. She was only 40 when she died.

Mahasweta Devi

Awarded the Jnanpith Award in 1996.
Recipient of Magsaysay Award in 1997.

Mahasweta Devi was born in 1926 in the city of Dacca in East Bengal (modern day Bangladesh). Her parents were noted literary figures of their time. Her father Manish Ghatak was a poet and novelist of repute and her mother Dharitri Devi was also a writer. She was a devoted social worker too. The literary home environment greatly influenced the young Mahasweta, who in her later life earned the name of a great writer especially for the down trodden and the weaker sections of society.

She began her early education in a school at Dhaka. After partition she and her family moved to West Bengal in India. She acquired her higher education at Vishvabharati University in Santiniketan, from where she did her B.A. (Hons.) in English. Later, she did her M.A. in the same subject from Calcutta University in 1963 as a private student.

Her contribution to the field of literature started very early. She wrote short stories in various magazines. Her first book *Jhansir Rani* (The Queen of Jhansi) was published in 1956, followed by a novel entitled *Nati* in 1957. In all her writings, she tried to depict the lives of ordinary men and women, particularly the Adivasi (tribal) people like the Santhals, Lodhas, Shabars and Mundas. She also tried to portray in her works the simple joys and sorrows of their life, their exploitation and sufferings and their condition of abject poverty.

Mahasweta Devi has published forty books including novels and short stories. Some of her well known works are—*Bioscoper Baksho, Aranyer, Adhikar, Hajar Churashir Ma, Chatti Munda*

O Tar Tir. She has also contributed to Economic and Political Weekly, Business Standard and other magazines.

In 1984, she retired from her job as an English lecturer at the Calcutta University to concentrate on her writing.

Her contributions to the field of literature won her several awards and laurels. She was awarded the Jnanpith Award for literature in 1996. She donated the prize money to a tribal welfare society. In 1997, she won the Magsaysay Award. In fact, she was the second Indian to receive this prestigious award. "It is good to win an award, but my life is getting more and more crowded and I am not getting time to write", she said when asked to comment on winning the award.

During the seventies, Mahasweta Devi also travelled widely in the rural areas of West Bengal and wrote a series of articles in a Bengali daily against the oppression of the tribal people of this region.

"I will continue to work for the tribals, non tribal poor and people in distress and write for them", she says.

Her book *Hajar Churashir Ma* (Mother of 1084) is the story of a upper middle class woman whose world is forever changed when her son is killed for his Naxalite beliefs. The book was made into a film by Govind Nihalani called "Hazaar Chaurasi Ki Ma". She earned much acclaim for works like *Araneyar Adhikar* (Rights of the Forest) based on the life of tribal freedom fighter Birsa Munda, Rudaali (now adapted by screen and stage directors).

For the Users

She is widely acknowldege as one of India's formost writers. Her work has won her several prestigious awards such as the Sahitya Akademi and Jhanpith awards, among several other literary honours. She was also awarded the Padma Shri for her work amongst dispossessed tribal communities.

REFERENCES

Bardhan, Kalpana, *Introduction of Women Outcastes Peasants and Rebels.* Los Angeles: University of California Press, 1990.

Bandypadhyay, Sanik Introduction, *Five Play,* Calcutta Seagull Book, 1986.

Spivak Gayatri Chakravorty *"The author in conversation"*, Imaginary, New York: Routledge Book, 1995.

Begum Akhtar

Gave her first performance at a charity show in aid of Bihar earthquake victims–1972.
She was a member of the Government of India's Cultural Delegation to Afghanistan where she gave several recitals–1963.
Awarded the Sangeet Natak Academy Award in1972.
Awarded Padma Bhushan Posthumosuly–1974.

Begum Akhtar was an eminent exponent of *ghazal, thumri* and *dadra.* She was a noted bhajan singer and an important exponent of the Poorabang thumree. She was born in a high-class family that was not musically inclined. However, at her uncle's insistence, she was sent to be trained under Ustad Imdad Khan, the great sarangi exponent, and later under Ata Mohammed Khan of Patiala. It was at Calcutta that she started learning music from classical stalwarts like Mohammad Khan, Abdul Waheed Khan and finally became the disciple of Ustad Jhande Khan Saheb.

In her quest, she was inspired by Jaddan Bai, a noted disciple of the great thumri singer, Moijuddin Khan (and mother of the late celebrated film actress Nargis). There was in her singing an incredible blend of all that was best in the Purabi and Punjab genres of light classical singing. Whatever the song-form, she had evolved her own individual and inimitable style of presenting it.

Her first public performance was at the tender age of 15. She was extremely fortunate when Sarojini Naidu attended a concert, that was organised for the aid of Bihar earthquake victims. This famous poet was full of praise for her. This further encouraged her to continue singing ghazals with more enthusiasm. She cut her first disc for the Megaphone Record Company at this time. Later on a number of gramophone records were released carrying her ghazals, dadras, thumris, etc.

Begum Akhtar also acted in a few Hindi movies in the thirties. The following two movies saw her active involvement. They were "Ek Din Ka Badsha" and "Nal Damyanti" in the year 1933. Like others of that era, she sang her songs herself in all her films. The other movies she acted in were Ameena (1934), Mumtaz Begum (1934), Jawaani Ka Nasha (1935), Naseeb Ka Chakkar (1935). In 1942, she acted in a film called "Roti". All gazals in the movie were sung by her.

In 1945, Begum Akhtar was married to barrister Ishtiaq Ahmed Abbasi and became known as Begum Akhtar. She acted on the stage as well. She immortalised her definitive style of singing a style that few have been able to match. She is rightly known as Malika-e-Ghazal.

Her voice matured with time, adding richness and depth. She sang ghazals and other light classical pieces. She was a regular performer on the All India Radio. She generally composed her own ghazals and most of her compositions were raag based.

Her last concert was held in Ahmedabad. She left for her heavenly abode on 30th October, 1974. She was posthumously awarded the Padma Bhushan.

She was widely travelled and ranked high among the foremost cultural ambassadors of India. She was awarded the Sangeet Natak Academy Award for vocal music in 1972. She sponsored and took part in many fund raising programmes. Her magical voice and delightful expressions were extremely popular with music lovers.

For the Users

One of the most popular musicians in the Indian subcontinent. An exponent of ghazal, thumri, dadra and bhajans. Her ghazals were a beautiful mix of Punjab and the Poorab style. Indeed, she was the queen of ghazals of her times. Her art was a vivid portrayal of the pure Lucknowi traditions of the Nawabs dating back to the 18th and 19th centuries.

REFERENCE

Nayar Sushila, Mankekas, Kamla (Ed), *Women Pioneers in India's Renaissance: As I Remember Her,* NBT, New Delhi, 2002.

P.T. Usha

Won a bronze medal at Cannanore for high jump in 1979.
Created a national record in the Kerala State Athletic Meet at Kottayam in Kerala in 1977.
Won four gold medals at National School Games at Nagpur in 1979.
Won two silver medals at the Asian Games in New Delhi in 1982.
Arjuna Award in 1983.
Awarded Padma Shri in 1985.
Won four gold and one silver at Seoul Olympics in 1986.

P.T. Usha was born on May 20, 1964 in Payyoli, located in Quilandi Taluk in Calicut district of Kerala. She was the second daughter of Irinjikal Puthenperayil Mannan Paithal and Thekke Vazhavalapil Lakshmi Amma. She was christened Usha by her maternal grandfather.

Every since her childhood, Usha was quite active. When she was one year old, she moved from one room to another as frequently as she could on an adventurous spree. She often climbed the wooden ladder to the second floor where the store room was located.

She started her education in Thrikottur Upper Primary School. When she was in class 4, one day E. Balakrishanan Nair, the school's Physical Teacher, saw Usha among the group of girls playing blind man's buff. At first, he could not believe his eyes when he saw the 10 year old blindfolded girl responding to the tests to participate in the local championships. Usha started practising for long jump under Thrikottur Nair. At the age of 11, she bagged the first place in all the four events she participated—100 metre, 200 metre, long jump and high jump. She also did well in her studies and was amongst the top three in her class.

Usha passed her class 7 with a first class and was admitted in Cannanore sports division. It was a sports-oriented school where meat and egg were part of the daily diet. A vegetarian by habit, she found it difficult to adjust. Despite, difficulty in adjusting to the food, Usha continued her education in this school. Under the guidance of Madhavan Nambiar, she received training in sports very scientifically. In 1977, at Cannanore, she won a bronze medal in high jump as well as 100 and 200 metres by equalling the then national record at the Kerala State School Meet. On December 17, 1997, she created national record in the Lera State Athletic Meet at Kottayam when she stormed past the 100 metres tape in an unbelievable timing of 13 seconds, thereby breaking the 13:1 seconds record time created in West Bengal. At the All India School Meet at Trivandrum, she played a major role in helping Kerala lift the Championship trophy for the first time in 23 years history. She was the junior champion with 10 points, had won the 100 metres gold and had helped the senior girls create a record in 100×4 metres relay in 51.7 seconds.

On March 1,1978, Usha won the junior 100 metres gold in 13.3 seconds and the next day cleared 1.35 metres to win the high jump gold. On the third day, she won the gold for 60 metres hurdles in 10.3 seconds. Thus, with four golds and one silver at the National Athletic Meet, Usha became a leading athlete of Kerala State.

At National School Games at Nagpur, held in the first week of January 1979, Usha won four gold medals. In 100 metres, by clocking 12.8 seconds she broke the three year old record of Reeta Deviah, and in half an hour went ahead and broke the four year old 200 metres record of Thangamma Antony by clocking 25.9 seconds. In February 1979, she represented Kerala at the National Games in Hyderabad where she clocked a record of 12.9 seconds in 100 metres. In 80 metres hurdles she broke the 13.6 second record of Jani Spix by clocking 13.5. In 200 metres, she broke the 26.4 second record of Maharashtra's Mertyn Fernandes by clocking 26 seconds. She also broke the 12.4 seconds of Tamil Nadu's Sandra Thomas in 80 seconds hurdles by clocking 12.2.

In spite of her hectric sports activities, Usha concentrated on her studies. In March 1979, she passed her matriculation. She wanted to become a doctor and joined Mercy College, Palghat, with natural science as optional subjects. After 2 years, she took a transfer to Providence College, Calicut, but had to discontinue her studies since the tight athletic schedules did not give her enough time to pursue her science studies, especially the practicals. From this college, however, she represented India at the Moscow Olympics where she was the youngest participant. Though Usha's performance was not memorable, she came back as an improved athlete. The awesome climate of the Olympics, the diehard competitive spirit of the Olympians, the higher standards of international athletes and the need to adapt to varying world conditions had all a very deep impact on her. Usha came back defeated, but not beaten. Usha did not give up. She continued her training under the guidance of Nambiar in Payyoli.

In January 1981, at the state Amateur Meet held at Irinjalakkuda in Trichur district, by clocking 24.6 seconds, Usha once again broke the 24.9 seconds record for 200 metres which stood in the name of Nani Radha. At Christ College, she was beaten in the 100 metres by her collegemate from Mercy College, Sreekumari, by an unbelievable timing of 12.2 seconds. In the final, she won the gold with a timing of 12.3 seconds.

On January 26, 1985, Usha was awarded Padma Shri by the President of India and she repaid the honour by starting her events in Chennai by breaking the meet record of 57.7 seconds in the 400 metres hurdles. She went on to win the 200 metres by equalling the meet record of 23.7 seconds and secured her name as the fastest woman in the country by bagging the gold at 11.8 seconds in 100 metres. She was also part of 4 x 400 metres and the 4×400 metres gold winning relay team of Kerala.

In 1986, in the Olympic Stadium at Seoul, South Korea's capital city, Usha won medal after medal, four gold and one silver, five in all, a record never before reached in the track scene of international athletics. The reception she got in her honour in India was tumultuous. Contributions from admirers from within the country and abroad poured in, while private companies and public sector undertakings in Kerala showered her with cash awards.

Her success had been gradual and continuous. Starting with two silver medals in the Delhi Asiad in 1982 she climbed the pinnacle of glory at Jakarta in 1985 and Seoul in 1986. It is significant to note that in 1982 though specialist doctors wrote her off as a cardiac case, yet within theree months she bounced back into Delhi Asiad with two silver medals. Athletics coach, publishing the British Amateur Athletics Board analysis of Olympic Track and Field, gave Usha a pat for balanced racing in the 400 metre hurdles.

On April 26, 1991, Usha married a sports enthusiast, Vengalli Veeti Shrinivasan, a Central Industrial Security Force Officer and state level Kabaddi player.

Recipient of Arjuna Award, P.T. Usha, the "Golden Girl" of India, is an athlete par excellence who climbed the top rung of glory at the age of 23 and became a legend for generations. A record number of appearances on the international track and field arena brought her four golds and 6 silvers in the Asian Games, 9 golds and 6 silvers from other meets, an Arjuna Award (1983) and Padma Shri. Winner of Adidas Golden Shoe for the best Asian Female Athlete for the year 1986, Usha has shown consistent improvement in her techniques. This has been the result of her systematic training, constant practice and preservance bracing through the most difficult and trying moments.

In fact, P.T. Usha's contribution to sports is unmatched. She was the winner of four gold medals and a silver medal in the Asiad 1986 held at Seoul. She created an Olympic sensation at Los Angles in 1984.

With the spirit of a fighter and a legendary zeal, P.T. Usha has realised her another dream with the Usha School of Athletics' she hopes to produce more world class women athletes and give to her motherland many more performers like her in the future.

The following is the chronological list of awards and achievements won by P.T. Usha:

Olympic Games	:	Los Angels, 1984 (4th in 400 metres hurdles) Atlanta, 1996 (Part of 4×400)
Asian Games	:	New Delhi, 1982 (Silver in 100m) Kuwait, 1983 (Silver in 200 m) Hiroshima, 1994 (4th in 200m) Seoul, 1986 (Gold in 200m) Jakarta, 1985 (Gold in 100 m, bronze in 4×100 relay) Beijing, 1990 (Silver in 400 m)
Asian Track and Field	:	Singapore, 1987 (400 m, 4 C relay) New Delhi, 1989 (Gold in 200 m, 4×100 m relay) Fukuoka, 1998 (Gold in 4×1400 m)
National Records	:	100 metres (11.39 seconds) 200 metres (23.25 seconds) 400 metres (51.61 seconds) 400 metres hurdles (55.42 seconds)

For the Users

The sprint queen broke all records in athletics and won the country great honour by winning several medals in international sports.

REFERENCE

Ahuja, M.L., *Glimpses of Some Great Indians,* Vikas Publishing House, New Delhi, 1997.

Santosh Yadav

Became a graduate from Maharani College, Jaipur in 1978.
1st successful experience in mountaineering was at a peak called 'White Needle' in Jammu and Kashmir. It was led by the Indo -Tibetan Border Security Force in 1989.
Alongwith the Indo- Taiwan Team she climbed a height of 25,170 feet and reached Sirsa, Kargil in 1990.
Successfully climbed Kanchenjunga in 1992.
Scaled the peak (Gauri Shanker) Mount Everest in 1992-93.
She is the only woman who has climbed Everest twice.

Santosh Yadav was born on 16th April 1964 in a small village Jonia in district Rewari in Haryana. She graduated in 1987 from Maharani College, Jaipur. Her subject was Economics. Since her childhood she was keenly interested in outdoor games and activities. It was her keen interest in outdoor activities that made her take part in N.C.C. since her school days. Her active participation in N.C.C.made her attend various camps organised by it. Her performance was highly appreciated and she was awarded 'C' grade which is considered to be a big achievement.

After doing an advance course from Uttar Kashi, she was very lucky to get herself associated with different mountaineering teams.

Her story of success begins from the year 1989 when a mountaineering team led by Director General Hukum Singh of the Indo- Tibetan Border Security Force was preparing to climb a peak in Jammu and Kashmir. Santosh approached him and expressed her desire. She was given permission to join the team. In this first venture she successfully climbed 'White Needle' a high peak in Kashmir. Later she became the only one to have successfully climbed the peak.

She was a member of the Indo-Taiwancse Saser Kangri-I (25, 170 *Pt.*) Expedition. She was one of the 18 summitters and achieved the distinction of being the first woman in the world to scale the highest peak in eastern Karakoram from the technically difficult West Face route. In recognition of her mountaineering potential she was appointed in the Indo-Tibetan Police force in November 1990. In 1991 she was selected as a member of the Indo-Japanese Kanchenjunga (East Route) Expedition and then she was chosen to join the Indian Pre-Everest Expedition to Mt. Kamet (25,446 Pt.) in which she remained in the fore front as a leading climber. Thereafter she succeeded in climbing the neighbouring Mt. Abi Ganmir (24, 130 Pt.) In 1992, she was proud to step on the summit of Mount Everest flying the Indian tricolour flag.

In 1993, as the deputy leader of the Indo-Napalese Women's Everest Expedition she achieved the rare distinction of becoming the first and the only woman in the world to climb Mt. Everest twice. She scaled Mt. Fujiyama, Japan's highest peak, on 25 June, 1995. In Februray 1998, she led an expedition to the Andes Mountains where her team hoisted the Indian Flag at the top of Mt. Cancagua in Argentina on 28 January, 1998 and did the country proud on its 50th year of independence. In March 1999, she led the Millennium Indian Everest (Kangshung Face) Expedition 1999 and bacame the first Indian to lead successfully an expedition to Mount Everest from its most dangerous and nearly impossible route 'Kangshung Face'.

Her love for mountaineering made Santosh leave her police job to pursue and promote mountaineering. She keenly promoted pilgrimage tour to Kailash and Mansarovar.

Santosh Yadav personally feels that the only way to achieve life time goal is to work very hard and understand the worth of time and value this life. This is the message she would like to give to the youth of India.

There were several reasons that helped her in achieving this mission. The constant encouragement provided by her parents and team leaders of different missions motivated her always. Further, strong will power, determination, ability to take risks, team spirit, her tough physique all these combined qualities were responsible for her remarkable achievement.

Though Santosh Yadav was successful in the above-mentioned missions, she had to face a lot of difficulties. Physically climbing heights lead to loss of appetite, fatigue, headache etc. However, it was her strong will power that saw her through. In an exclusive interview to *'Education Times'* she said that mountaineering had come to her as a natural gift and now she was working towards the promotion of adventure sports.

For the Users

This is the story of a woman who attained the second position of conquering the highest mountain peak Mt. Everest and set an example for other women.

REFERENCE

R.K. Bhatnagar, Adapted from 'Beyond the last blue mounain', Exclusive Interview to *Education Times,* 16 April, 2001.

Jyotirmoyee Sikdar

Won the following Awards: Two gold medals in Bangkok Asian Games–1998.
Arjuna Award–1996.
Rajiv Khel Ratna Award in 1999.
Padma Shri–2003.

Jyotirmoyee Sikdar belonged to a humble family from Debagram in Nadia distruct of West Bengal. Her father Gurudas Sikdar was a school teacher. He was also a member of the Communist Party of India. Jyotirmoyee started participating at a young age in athletics, while she was still in high school. After finishing school, her coach Satyaram Roy, brought her to a town near, Calcutta. It was Satyada's support that made her continue her interst in athletics. She first tasted success when she won the gold medal in the All India Universities Athletics Meet. Since then she has never looked back.

She met her husband Avtar at a sports camp in Patiala in 1993. Her husband meant a lot to her because of his faith in her capabilities and was a great source of encouragement.

Some of her great achievements in the field of sports were winning two individual gold medals in the 800 and 1500 metres at the 'Bangkok Asian Games' in 1998. Before the game started, she said in her own words, "I am sure to win a medal in the Asian Games but the question is its colour". She was unable to participate at the 'Olympics' in Sydney as she had an injury which forced her to drop out and then she subsequently announced her retirement. Once again in her own words she said, "My decision had been prompted by various factors other than just injuries. I tried to fight all odds but soon realised that I was fighting a losing battle."

Meanwhile, the Asian games success brought with it some prosperity. The West Bengal Government promptly allotted her a plot of land in Salt Lake in Calcutta. She also received a cheque of Rs. 2,00,000 from the Chief Minister Jyoti Basu.

Sikdar's contribution to athletics was recognised by the Government and subsequently she won several awards such as— 'Arjuna Award' in 1996, 'Rajiv Khel Ratna Award' in 1999 and finally the highest civilian award i.e. 'Padma Shri' in 2003. In fact, she was the first athlete from Bengal to have got the Padma Shri. Sikdar said that she planned to start an academy to groom young budding talents.

She decided to plunge into politics. She was CPI (M)'s nominee from Ranaghat (west) for assembly elections.

For the Users

The well known athlete overcame poverty to emerge as a leading athlete of the country. She won laurels in various international meets.

REFERENCES

The Hindustan Times, Sunday, 20 December, 1998.

The Times of India, Monday, 27 January, 2003.

Kiran Bedi

Won NCC Best Cadet Officers Award in 1968.
Won Asian Lawn Tennis Championship in 1972.
Served as a Lecturer in Political Science in Khalsa College for Women, Amritsar in 1970-72.
Joined the Indian Police Service and subsequently became the first woman to do so- 1972.
Led the Republic Day Parade in 1973.
Awarded the Police Medal for Gallantry in 1979.
Won the Seventh Jawaharlal Nehru National Solidarity Award. Declared women of the year in 1980.
Did her LLB from Delhi University in 1988.
Received the Magsaysay Award for Government Service. First Woman Police Officer to have won it .
Nehru Fellowship Awarded in 1997.
Nehru Memorial Fund (Subject: Tihar Prison Management).

Kiran Bedi was born on 9th June, 1949 at Amritsar. Her Parents Parkash Lal and Prem Lata were keen supporters of women's education and were unconventional in their thinking and attitude. They wanted to educate their daughters so that they could carve a space for themselves in society and think equally and independently. It is because of their encouragement and constant support that she successfully did her initial schooling and graduation from Amritsar. She later did her post-graduation from Punjab University, Chandigarh. In her own words she said, "My father was a visionary, and my mother very determined, hard working and caring. Both had a dream to see all their daughters grow up strong and stand on their own feet. At my home everyday was inspirational, a training ground for the future......."

Kiran excelled both at school and at tennis, a family passion. In 1972, at the age of twenty two, she won the women's lawn tennis championship of Asia. The same year, she entred the Police Academy and, in 1974, became the first woman to enter the elite Indian Police Service. Assigned to the capital city of Delhi, she rose rapidly in the ranks, winning national acclaim and a presidential award in 1978 by single handedly driving off a band of club and sword wielding demonstrators with her police baton.

As Deputy Commissioner of police in Delhi's West and North Districts, Kiran posted her constables in blue and white 'beat boxes' where citizens could consult them daily. She redirected former bootleggers. who made and sold alcohol illicitly, to honest livelihood by arranging friendly loans and assistance. At her own initiative, she set up women's peace committees to promote neighbourhood harmony. It is significant to note that her efforts bore fruit as community participation rose. Observing the link between drug addiction and chronic criminality, Kiran set up community supported detoxification clinic, a model she later developed for wider application as Deputy Director of the Narcotics Control Bureau.

As New Delhi Traffic Chief, she meticulously regulated traffic at the 1982 Asian Games.

The other significant assignment was when she became Inspector General of prisons in 1993. She took charge of Tihar Jail, India's largest prison complex. Her jail reforms won her laurels. It is because of her initiatives that its immates follow a positive attitude towards work, study and play. Illiterate prisoners learnt to read and write. Others earned higher degrees by cooperating with collegues. In prison workshops, prisoners kept their skills tuned and earned wages to save in Tihar's new bank. Through their panchayats (elected councils), inmates shared the responsibility of community discipline and of organising game and entertainment. In yoga classes they learn meditation techniques to conquer anger and improve concentration. Their complaints placed in the mobile petition box got directly addressed by the top senior officials.

In other words, Kiran firmly believes in rehabilitation of criminals rather than punishing them.

Despite being extremely busy in performing her duties to the best of her abilities, Kiran Bedi obtained a degree in law from Delhi University. Later, she acquired a doctorate, in 1993 from Delhi University.

Her close association with Tihar Jail made her apply for Jawaharlal Nehru Fellowship. She was lucky and was awarded the 'Nehru Fellowship' in 1994-97. Her subject was "Tihar Prison Management." In her own words she said, "For me, writing about my prison work is like writing a scripture. Prison work had become a form of worship for me. Having attained this edifying position, I am presently in no 'state of mind' to come down to 'base' affairs a traffic prosecution here or busting a gang there (as it feels for me now). My heart now lies in the 'human resource management'. Currently, she is posted as Police Advisor in the U.N. Peace Keeping Department. She has also been honoured with the U.N. Medal for her outstanding service. In fact, Kiran Bedi was felicitated along with 22 other officers for serving with the world body.

For the Users

This is the story of a woman who became the country's first woman police officer. Her contribution to the service has earned her national and international fame and she has received many awards for her service.

REFERENCES

Ahuja, M.L., *Glimpses of Some Great Indians*. Vikas Publishing House, New Delhi.

Dangwal, Parmesh, *I Dare: Kiran Bedi: A Biography,* U.B.S

Deccan Chronicle, 29 May, 2004.

Menon, Ritu (Ed), *Women Who Dared,* NBT, New Delhi, 2002.

Conclusion

The proposed book includes names of eminent women who have contributed in different fields. The different paths they adopted for achieving their goals is an inspiring story for all children. These women were true role models in the period they belonged to and continue to be even today. The different fields in which they excelled demystify certain notional beliefs that women are suited only for doing feminine roles.

Their achievements in different fields portray that given an opportunity women can perform and even excel in all fields. Further, it also highlights that in the Indian context women enjoy a status i.e. a mix between the ascribed and achieved status.

The book can be used by textbook writers and teachers for enhancing self esteem and self confidence of the girl child. Perhaps, it can also help in kindling in the girl child a dream for participating in courses and professions which were considered non-traditional and unconventional for them earlier.

Appendix

Some Messages for Girls and Women

1. "By education, I mean an all round drawing out of the best in the child, women and men; body, mind and spirit".

Mahatma Gandhi

2. "One skips to school to play read and write but many children work hard day and night. All children must have equal opportunities to grow and realise their abilities".

Education for All : 2000
UNICEF, Lodi Estate, New Delhi

3. "I want to go to school" is her silent plea but I have to support the family. We must help to make her dream come true. The girl's right to education is long overdue".

Education For All : 2000
UNICEF, Lodi Estate, New Delhi

4. "Education for All is the country's goal towards which we all must play a role. Every educated person should educate some more. India's great glory we must restore".

5. "To call women the weaker sex is a libel; it is man's injustice to woman. If by strength is meant brute strength, then, indeed, woman is less brute than man. If by strength is meant moral power, then woman is immeasurably man's superior. Has she not greater intuition, is she not more self sacrificing, has she not greater powers of endurance, has she not greater courage? Without her, man could not be. If non violence is the law of our being, the future is with woman. Who can make a more effective appeal to the heart than woman".

Mahatma Gandhi

6. "If human development is not engendered, it becomes endangered."

Human Development Report (UNDP)

7. "Progressive womanhood is a sure symbol of a progressive nation. Enslaved, illiterate and ignorant womanhood is a no less a sure symbol of a degenerate, backward or a dependent country....."

Sir Vithaldas Thackersey

8. "Child marriage is a crime against half of our beloved humanity. Its monstrousness lies in the fact that it opens the flood gate of other corruption".

9. "If women's power was only organised and mobilised, it would transform the world".

Vidyagauri Nilkant

10. "The 73rd and 74th Constitutional Amendments (1993) guarantee women a minimum 1/3 representation in all local bodies both in the rural and urban areas and also reserve, 1/3 of all posts of Chairperson for women".

11. "O Lord, why have you not given woman the right to conquer her destiny? Why does she have to wait head bowed by the roadside, waiting with tired patience hoping for a miracle in the morrow".

Rabindranath Tagore

12. "The constitution not only grants equality to women, but also empowers the state to adopt measures of positive discrimination in favour of women". Education can be an effective tool for women's empowerment, the parameters of which are:

— enhancing self-esteem and self confidence of women/ building a positive image of women by recognising their contribution to the society, polity and the economy;
— developing ability to think critically;

— fostering decision and action through collective process;
— enabling women to make informed choices in areas like education, employment and health, especially reproductive health;
— ensuring equal participation in development processes;
— providing information, knowledge and skills for economic independence;
— enhancing access to legal, literacy and information relating to their rights and entitlements in society with a view to enhance their participation on equal footing in all areas.

Programmes of Action 1992

13. "If only the women of the world would come together they could display such heroic non violence as to kick away the atom bomb like a mere ball. Women have been so gifted by God. If an ancestral treasure, lying buried in a corner of the house unknown to the members of the family, were suddenly discovered, what a celebration it would occasion. Similarly women's marvellous power is lying dormant. If the women of Asia wake up, they will dazzle the world. My experiment in non violence would be instantly successful if I could secure women's help".

Mahatma Gandhi

14. "If we do not have the courage to choose to live in a particular way, even though we could live that way if we so choose, can it be said that we do not have freedom to live that way, i.e. the corresponding capability?"

Amartya Sen

15. "The habit of looking upon marrige as the sole economic refuge for women will have to go before women can have any freedom. Freedom. depends on economic conditions even more than political, and even if a woman is not economically free and self-earning she will have to depend on the husband or someone else, and dependents are never free."

Jawaharlal Nehru

16. "I have completed my mission of interacting with 100,000 school children across the length and breadth of the nation. Wherever I went, be it Arunachal Pradesh, Nagaland, Madhya Pradesh, Gujarat, Karnataka or any other part of India, the voice of the youth is unique and strong in articulating their vision and dream. Everyone dreams of living in a prosperous India, a happy India and peaceful India. The combination of prosperity and peace always comes together. When all three of them converge on to India, then India will truly be a Developed Nation."

Dr. A.P.J. Abdul Kalam
President of India

17. "Girls of Today Pride of Tomorrow Invest in her as she is the Nations' Asset".

Gouri Srivastava

18. "A Girl Child has the Right to Survival, Protection, Participation and Development."

Gouri Srivastava

19. "Empowerment of Girl Child, Responsibility of All."

Gouri Srivastava

20. "The key to Sustainable Human Development is Women's Empowerment."

Gouri Srivastava

21. "Women's Development is a key to Global Peace, Prosperity and Harmony".

Gouri Srivastava

22. "Provision of literacy and skills to girls are means for strengthening Human Resource Development."

Gouri Srivastava

23. Sex Ratio in India : 1901-2001

Census Year	*Sex Ratio (Female per 1,000 male)*
1901	972
1911	964
1921	955
1931	950
1941	945
1951	946
1961	941
1971	930
1981	934
1991	927
2001	933

Source : Census of India, 2001, p.85.

"Where are the Missing Girls Court her in she is the Nations Wealth and Asset".

Gouri Srivastava

24. Literacy Rate : 2001

Male:	75.85
Female:	54.16

Source : Census of India 2001.

25. "If you educate a woman you educate a family, So invest in her".

Gouri Srivastava

26. "Girls' Education, an Agenda to be Fulfilled For Well being of the Nations".

Gouri Srivastava

27. "Girls Education, Lasting Benefits To Future Generation."

Gouri Srivastava

28. "Strengthen the Foundation of Girls Education as the Returns are Bountiful."

Gouri Srivastava

29. "Cherish Cultural Diversities, End Gender Disparities."

Gouri Srivastava

30. "Educate a Girl Child for a Better Future."

Gouri Srivastava

31. "Care and Nurture the Girl Child as she is The Harbinger of a healthier and prosperous Nation."

Gouri Srivastava

32. "Educate her as she will spread The light of knowledge."

Gouri Srivastava

33. "Give her strength to negotiate and communicate and she will help her species to participate."

Gouri Srivastava

34. "Educate her for she will educate the generations to come."

Gouri Srivastava

35. "Girls Education the Agenda of the Millennium."

Gouri Srivastava

36. "Ensure her survival as she will ensure the survival of the humanity."

Gouri Srivastava

37. "Give her the means and she will give you the results."

Gouri Srivastava

38. "Bridging gender disparities in education is a sure step for attaining Education for All."

Gouri Srivastava

39. "Have faith in her as she can do wonders."

Gouri Srivastava

40. "Gender Justice, Harmony and Peace are goals for Sustainable Human Development."

Gouri Srivastava

41. "Equality is the goal achieve it: Equality is the process, stress on it."

Gouri Srivastava

42. Gender perspective in planning is a sure step to end disparity and discrimination.

Gouri Srivastava

Bibliography

Ahuja, M.L., *Glimpses of Some Great Indians,* Vikas Publishing House, New Delhi, 1997.

An Album of Indian Writers: Issued on the Occasion of Frankfurt World Book Fair, 1986, Sahitya Academi, New Delhi, 1986.

Bagchi, K. Ashoke, *Great Women of Science,* Konarak Publishers, New Delhi, 1994.

Basu, Aparna, *Mridula Sarabai: A Rebel with a cause,* Oxford University Press, New Delhi.

Basu, Aparna Renuka Ray (1940-1997): *Roshini, Journal of AIWC,* July, 1997, New Delhi.

Bhavan's Journal, Vol. 35, No. 21, 15 June 1989, Bombay.

Bhavan's Journal, 31 August 2004, Vol. J, No. 2, Bharatiya Vidya Bhavan, Mumbai.

Bandyopadhyay, Sanik, "*Introduction: Five Play,* Calcutta Seagull Book, 1986.

Bardhan, Kalpana, *Introduction of Women, Outcastes, Peasants and Rebels,* Los Angeles: University of California Press, 1990.

Bhatnagar, R.K., Adapted from 'Beyond the Last Blue Mountain', Exclusive Interview to *Education Times,* 16 April, 2001.

Cour, Ajeet & Cour (Ed): *Aparna Directory of Indian Women Today,* 1976, International Publication, New Delhi, 1970.

Chawla, Navin, *Mother Teresa : The Authorised Biography.*

Deccan Chronide, 29 May, 2004.

Dandavate, Madhu, *Architects of Modern India,* V.N.O. key Felicitation Committee, Bombay, 1989.

Dangwal, Parmesh, *I Dare: Kiran Bedi: A Biography.*

Datta, S.C, *Five Eminent Women.* Anmol Publication, New Delhi, 1993.

Excerpts from *Past Forward.* as told to Gouri Ramnarayan, Oxford University Press, 1997.

Frontline, 31 December, 2004.

Hameeduddin, Mahmood, *The Kaleidoscope of Indian Cinema,* New Delhi, East West Press, 1974.

Hindustan Times, Persona, 12th December, 2000.

Jain, C.K., *Women Parliamentarians in India,* Surjeet Publication, New Delhi, 1993.

Loojtilla, Gyula, *Amrita Shergil & Hungary,* Allied Publishers Private Limited, New Delhi, 1981.

Menon, Ritu, (Ed): *Women Who Dared,* NBT, New Delhi, 2002.

Misra, Sosheda, *Some Dancers of India.* New Delhi, 1972.

Mishra, Bibhuti, "Sanjukta Elevated and Enriched Odissi", *The Indian Express,* 25 June, 1997, New Delhi.

Nayar, Sushila and Mankekar, Kamla, *Women Pioneers in India's Renaissance:* ASI Remember Her, National Book Trust, India, 2002.

Rajadhyaksha Ashish, Willemen, Paul, *Encyclopaedia of Indian Cinema,* London, British Film Institute, Oxford University Press, 1994.

Singh, Shanta, Serbjeet, "*The Eternal Shishya*" *Hindustan Times.* 5 July, 1997.

Spivak Gayatri Chakravorty, *The Author in Conversation, Imaginary,* New York, Routledge Book, 1995.

The Hindustan Times, Sunday, 20 December, 1998.

The Times of India, Monday, 27 Jaunary, 2003.

Upadhyay, Madhu, *Profiles in Creativity,* Sudhindra Offset Process, Bangalore, 1990.

Volume on Diamond Jubilee 1927-87, All India Women's Conference, New Delhi.

INDEX